OUT OF THE DARKNESS

THE SPIDER JONES STORY

To The Staff
of Pickering

Library

[signature]

Published by ECW PRESS
2120 Queen Street East, Suite 200, Toronto, Ontario, Canada M4E 1E2

NATIONAL LIBRARY OF CANADA CATALOGUING IN PUBLICATION DATA

Jones, Spider
The Spider Jones story /Spider Jones and Michael Hughes.

ISBN 1-55022-603-7

1. Jones, Spider.   2. Radio broadcasters – Canada – Biography.
3. Boxers (Sports) – Canada – Biography.
4. Lecturers – Canada – Biography.   I. Hughes, Michael, 1947–   II. Title.

PN1991.4.J65A3 2003   348.54'092   C2003-902417-2

Front cover photo by Marko Shark

The publication of *Out of the Darkness* has been generously supported by the Canada
Council, the Ontario Arts Council, and the Government of Canada through the Book
Publishing Industry Development Program. **Canada**

DISTRIBUTION

CANADA: Jaguar Book Group, 100 Armstrong Ave., Georgetown ON L7G 5S4

UNITED STATES: Independent Publishers Group, 814 North Franklin Street,
Chicago, Illinois 60610

PRINTED AND BOUND IN CANADA

ECW PRESS
ecwpress.com

OUT OF THE DARKNESS

THE SPIDER JONES STORY

Spider Jones and Michael Hughes

ECW PRESS

Prologue   vii

CHAPTER 1   Selling Wolf Tickets   1

CHAPTER 2   Ma and Dad   13

CHAPTER 3   Hey, Buckwheat!   25

CHAPTER 4   The Angel of Death   31

CHAPTER 5   Sewer Rats   39

CHAPTER 6   Getting Clean for the Lord   45

CHAPTER 7   The Lunch Bag Bandit   55

CHAPTER 8   My Singing Debut   65

CHAPTER 9   Hitting Back!   73

CHAPTER 10   The Ding-Dong Class   83

CHAPTER 11   Big Jim   93

CHAPTER 12   A Great Thief   103

CHAPTER 13   Smokers   113

CHAPTER 14   Living Large   123

CHAPTER 15   New Business Development   133

CHAPTER 16   Tyrone and Buster   143

CHAPTER 17   The Greatest   151

CHAPTER 18   Ali-Chuvalo I — 1966   163

CHAPTER 19   The Most Feared Address in America   173

CHAPTER 20   Murder City Burns   183

CHAPTER 21   The Death of Blackbottom   191

CHAPTER 22   Running with the Panthers   201

CHAPTER 23   Smokin' Tex   211

CHAPTER 24   You Are Everything . . .   225

CHAPTER 25   Stand by Me   239

CHAPTER 26   Radio Dreams Reborn   249

CHAPTER 27   The Spider's Web   259

Epilogue   271

Acknowledgements   277

Prologue

For most of my life, success was a goal that hurt to think about. Hurt so much I wouldn't let myself dream the dream. But dreams die hard when they're good ones, and my dream kept at me my entire life. Thirty years after I dropped out of school, when I was hired on at TALK640 radio in Toronto in 1999, I had reached the top in the radio business: the only black person in Canada with his own prime-time radio show, *The Spider's Web*. "Out of the darkness" had become my life's theme — my internal battle cry. I had done the undoable!

TALK640 was located on the top two floors of a thirty-storey office tower on Yonge Street in north Toronto, North America's third-largest media market. But even when I got there, satisfaction was undermined by those damn beasts that had stalked me my whole life — lack of self-confidence and lack of self-esteem. Our studios looked south, toward downtown Toronto, and after my show I would sometimes go to the semidarkness of the vacant business offices just to look out over the city and savour how far I'd come. Way down below was Yonge Street, all lit up and sparkling like Canada's Broadway with evening traffic crawling along like kids' toys, and there I was, up high in the clouds and one of the best-known radio personalities in town: the Prince of the City to my listeners.

But staring out those tinted windows, I could see something other than the view. I could see *myself*, my own features reflected back ghostlike in the glass. I stared into the eyes, and I saw what others didn't see. I saw lingering old doubts trying to shake me up, to gnaw away at my confidence like the big fat sewer rats of my Mercer Street boyhood. Sometimes I couldn't fully believe that I had really made it from the negativity that poverty and racism pound into you to this position at the top.

On a particularly cold February night in 2001, my on-air guest was to be former Buffalo Bills quarterback Jim Kelly. But even as I went down the hall to meet Jim, I was aware of the subtle racism that always surrounded me as I walked past shiny platinum records and pictures of smiling rock stars in expensive chrome frames. Some of the most famous people in the world have been through these studios, but there were no black faces among the photos. Not that there aren't enough famous black music stars; they just didn't show up on those walls. I knew that thought never struck my coworkers. I was the only black person on the staff and the only one who'd come out of poverty in the realest sense of the word. I was from another world.

Jim approached, and we shook hands. He was larger than I'd expected. Many quarterbacks are smaller, more compact for mobility, but Jim was taller than I was. I'd also heard that he was arrogant, but I didn't sense arrogance. I did sense pain. Jim had come to talk about his son, who was dying, and I felt much compassion for the man.

In those days, Jim was waging a battle against an insidious killer called Krabbe's disease which had targeted his ten-year-old son, Hunter. Krabbe's is a rare degenerative neurological condition that slowly erodes sight, hearing, and, over time, all mental faculties. Death is the end result as the mind completely shuts down. That night we weren't going to get into football stuff. Jim had heard enough of those tired, dumb-assed, old questions about why the Bills hadn't been able to win one of those Super Bowls. That night we were going to talk about a disease that attacks children and what can be done about it. How parents like the Kellys deal with it.

We walked back to the studio area, and Jim slid into the leather guest chair beside mine at the control console, my work area. He pulled some rumpled notes from his blue denim shirt, and fatigue was written all over his face. This was his fifteenth stop of the day. Welcome to the reality of promotion. Jim was there with the single-minded purpose of promoting Hunter's Hope Foundation Hockey Tournament.

The prompting voice of my producer came through my earphones: "Time to deliver the goods, guys. . . ."

I hit the on-air button, and it was showtime!

"Helloooooo, Big City, and good evening, Nighthawks. This is the boss of the hot sauce, the loveable one, the cat who brought the nitty-gritty back to the city, Spider Jones coming at you 'til nine o'clock tonight. Lots to talk about. You have just entered *The Spider's Web*, also known as *The Land of Outspokendry*, where the official language is telling it like it is, so get ready, teddy! My special guest tonight is NFL great and former Buffalo Bills quarterback Jim Kelly. . . ."

And so another show began.

When I wrapped up Kelly's portion of the show, we arranged to meet later out at Don Cherry's arena — the Hershey Centre — in nearby Mississauga to shoot some footage with Don and other celebrities to promote Jim's upcoming hockey tournament.

After Jim left, I finished the final hour with my usual mix

of sports talk, trivia, hot topics of the day, and call ins. Then I signed off and started the drive to Don's. It was a typical February night in Toronto: the roads were icy and treacherous, and the wind was lashing snow across the hood of my car. I shivered as old memories of frigid winters past began to creep in. Memories I try so hard to put behind me. To this day, I *hate* the cold. I've never gotten over the fact that the cold haunted me as a kid and killed my little brother, Dennis, in his bed. When Dennis died, it set off a chain of events that sent me spiralling into a darkness of depression and low self-esteem that took me most of my life to come out of.

To my wife, and best friend Jackie.
— Spider Jones

To my inspiration . . . my daughter, Jessica.
— Michael Hughes

Selling Wolf Tickets

Many people trade on their misery, but I think it's pretty well documented that poor black folks in North America in the 1950s had few advantages and plenty of real privations. Simple things, such as central heating, were beyond my family when I was a kid. Come early November, the cold set in in our little frame house, and it never loosened its grip till springtime. No matter how much coal Dad stoked into the old iron stove in the kitchen, long before dawn the fire died out and took any heat with it. Then the cold was enough to kill your spirit. Or a little boy.

We knew that Dennis was sick, that he had pneumonia, because my mother had explained to us what that was. But words like "pneumonia" didn't mean much at that age. Pneumonia was just some sort of bad cold that caused a runny nose and coughing. That was a long way from dying. I *always* had a runny nose and a cough in those days. I'd also had pneumonia and had spent a month in a hospital. I too had almost died of it. So sickness wasn't new to us.

But death was. I had no sense or understanding of death at six years old. Dennis's crib was right next to the bed my brothers and I shared, and little Dennis died less than two feet from where we were sleeping.

The rest of us kids were lucky that we didn't freeze to death that night as well. Ma said it was the coldest winter since the 1930s. Ma and Dad tried hard to keep us warm that winter; night after night, Ma piled blankets and old quilts on us, and Dad loaded up the stove with coal and put burlap sacks along the bottom of the kitchen door so frigid air couldn't blow straight in. But the fire in the stove lasted only a few hours, and the cold seeped in anyway, so my father would get up before sunrise in a house like an icebox to restart the fire as we shivered in our early morning beds. Often the first thing we saw in the morning was our misted breath in the air above our piles of stinking blankets.

One of my chores was to fetch coal from the back shed for the stove. When we ran out, Ma or Dad would lay a two-dollar bill on me and send me to the coal yard about a mile away. It wasn't the distance that bothered me as much as the gangs of tough white kids that prowled the area looking for black boys like me. They loved to use us as target practice. In the summer, it was rocks or ball bearings rocketed from slingshots. In the winter, it was hard-packed ice balls. When you're pulling a sleigh with a seventy-five-pound burlap bag of coal, it's tough to duck an ice ball, and I took many off the side of my head. I had to pass through three different hostile turfs to reach the coal yard.

Some of the bigger dudes ran protection rackets; if you wanted to pass without trouble, you had to pay a toll. I could

never afford to pay it; I needed the money for the coal. So
usually I took the long way to avoid them, the back lanes
behind the factories and along the railway tracks.

On that bitter January evening in 1953, it had been snow-
ing for hours, and the drifts were high along the unploughed
back lanes, so I was forced to take to the front streets. About
halfway to the coal yard, I ran into Red Turner and his gang
hanging in front of the variety store. There was no way
around them. Red was a mean kid a year or two older than
me, a whole lot bigger and, in those days, a whole lot
tougher. He demanded my money. I lied, said I was broke.
But these were poor kids too who knew the game. Red knew
where I was going. You didn't go out into the cold after dark
for nothing, and you didn't get coal for free. Red called me a
dumb-assed nigger and sucker-punched me. When I went
down, his boys put the boots to me. They robbed me of the
two dollars and took my little raggedy-assed red sled as well.

I returned home empty-handed, crying, bleeding, and
with a sharp pain in my ribs. I explained through tears what
had happened, but the one thing I didn't do was give up
Red's name. That was one street code I knew enough not to
break, even at that age.

My father, by nature laid-back and easygoing, went
berserk. He hated bullies. He grabbed his coat and lit out
with fire in his eyes to look for them dudes. If he'd gotten his
hands on them, it would have been ugly. Probably would
have brought more trouble down on our heads than it was
worth. But he never did find them, though he did manage to
find my sled a couple of blocks away, ditched in a snowbank
where I'd been attacked.

By the time all the commotion had settled down, the coal

yard was closed. Dad looked in the coal scuttle beside the stove. There were a few chunks at the bottom but not enough to last through the night. He loaded the few pieces in before turning in and prayed for the best. I guess he hoped, being a devout Baptist, that he might have some special pull with God. Of course, he didn't have special pull with *anybody*, and by midnight the stove was out. The cold came at the house like a long-tongued monster; it licked in through cracks in the floor, under the windowpanes and doorframes, and through cracks in the walls.

When I awoke the next morning, Ma was tending to Dennis, still a baby at eighteen months. His nose was all crusty and running, and he was wheezing like a busted accordion. He could hardly squeeze a breath. I remember her look of concern as she called the doctor.

Doc Chatters was a tall, stooped, gentlemanly man from the West Indies. He always wore a rumpled suit, a tie loosely knotted and a little crooked, and a black bowler hat. He carried a small, battered black leather case with him. He was even lighter complected than my mother was, though he was considered black. He considered himself black, and all the blacks called on him, but to look at him many people thought he was white.

After closing down his small office, Doc stopped by. He had an odd speech impediment. He'd bob his head and speak through his nose as if he had a nasal problem. That day he put his stethoscope against Dennis's chest. You could see that Dennis was struggling to breathe. His face was bluish, and every breath was an effort. Doc said simply, "Ahhhnnnh, boy's pretty sick. Boy's pretty sick. If that baby don't improve by tomorrow, git him straight to the hospital." That was the sum of the treatment he was able to dispense, and he packed up his bag and left.

But there was no tomorrow for Dennis. He passed away that night in his crib.

The next morning, before dawn, we were jolted from our sleep by my ma's pitiful screams. "He's gone! He's gone! Clarence! Oh, God, Clare, our baby's gone!" My mother was standing next to the crib holding Dennis to her chest and sobbing convulsively. "Oh, God," she pleaded, "please bring back my baby! Pleeeease!"

All us kids began to cry even though we didn't fully understand what was happening. All I knew about death was what we'd heard in church, that it had something to do with heaven and clouds and angels and rousing gospel music. But even though we didn't know how final death was, we were stunned by my mother's uncharacteristic display of grief. It was heartbreaking to watch Ma rock back and forth cradling the body of our little brother.

Then Dad too began to weep. It was the first time I saw my dad cry.

Later that morning a hollow-cheeked man sent by the city showed up dressed in a faded black suit and a rumpled old trenchcoat. He carried a well-scuffed black leather case. He tossed Dennis's little body into the case as if it was a rag doll going to the Salvation Army resale store. That hit me hard. It was so insensitive. I guess the man had dealt with so much death that he'd become desensitized. If removing Dennis's remains was meant to be a comfort, it wasn't; it felt more like an assault. There were no consoling or kind words from this man. Just cold efficiency: "Sign here, ma'am." A bit of warmth toward my parents would have gone a long way in our hurtin' home.

I think my problems in life were triggered the night Dennis died. It was when my nightmares began.

But another childhood event was to cause me an even greater setback. It was the night when, at age twelve, I first dreamt of becoming a radio personality. I still think of it as the night the dream was born . . . and died.

It was 1958, and I was a thin, scruffy kid with a don't-mess-with-me attitude, the kind that struck terror in the hearts of decent white folks everywhere. 'Course, I wasn't big enough yet to strike terror in the hearts of my own people. They were too inured to terror. It would be another year or two before I was big enough, tough enough, and mean enough to start selling wolf tickets to my own people with any conviction. Selling wolf tickets is street slang for fixing a fierce expression on your face — even if you don't feel especially fierce that day — just to give off the message that you're not to be messed with.

At twelve, I was just coming out of a dark period that had begun when Dennis died. My passivity, my backwardness, my always feeling like a victim was starting to change. I was turning a corner, becoming more assertive, more determined. I even began to feel a glimmer of confidence.

That summer the manager of the Windsor Arena, a fellow named Cito, offered me two dollars a night to help sweep out the hallways and dressing rooms after events. In 1958, two dollars a night was big for a twelve-year-old kid. It made me feel like a real working man. So I began.

I no sooner started than my dream began to take shape. One of the first big rock 'n' roll shows to come through town

that year was Buddy Holly and his Crickets. I watched the
whole show from the back of the arena leaning on my
broom, and *man!* there sure was something about Buddy
that captivated everyone who saw him, including me. I'd
never felt so alive as I did listening to the music that day.
Even though by today's standards it was a pretty low-decibel
show, the sounds still vibrated through the floor and gave
me a chill that came through my sneakers and right up my
backbone. I fell under the spell of live music shows that day.

After the show, the place emptied out quickly, and Cito
told me to get my butt moving on clean up, and he sent me
to the dressing rooms to start. The arena was also used as a
roller-skating rink, and the rooms were always a mess by the
end of the week. My head was still in the clouds as I broomed
out the first dressing room, dumped all the wrappers and
cups into the big tin garbage can, and dragged the can scraping down the hall to the next room. It was going to take me
a long time to come down from the excitement of the show.
I pushed the door open to the next dressing room, and there
he was — Buddy Holly! He was just pulling his things
together and getting ready to clear out.

I could only stare.

Buddy glanced over and said, "I'm almost done, son."

I eased inside with my broom and dustpan, but I still
couldn't help staring, and he could tell I was starstruck. He
asked me my name, just to be nice. I told him "Chuck."
He nodded, put his foot on the bench, and reached down
to tie up his shoe. He was dressed *sharp!* Smart, speckled
black sports jacket, creased billowy pants, red satin shirt,
black shiny shoes. And he had on those thick-framed glasses
he became so famous for.

He asked, "So, did you like the show, Chuck?"

The floodgates opened. What a thrill! This rock 'n' roll idol took time to make small-talk with a wide-eyed kid with a broom in his hand. I was in heaven! This was one wonderful cat! I knew he was just trying to put me at ease, but I started talking in a stream. I told him how much his music had moved me, how great the performance had been, how much I loved rock 'n' roll and rhythm 'n' blues, how wonderful it was to actually meet the man himself, and that I even sang gospel music in church with my dad sometimes. I got it all out in one breath.

Buddy smiled. He was so warm and sincere. He'd probably seen it a thousand times — kids falling under the spell. He grabbed up a kind of gym bag with some stage clothes in it and said, "Son, ain't nothing better than singing music. If you love music, dream big. You never know where it can take you." And then he was gone.

I watched him head down the hall, and a new dream flickered. When he died the next spring in that damnable plane crash, I cried and mourned like I would for family.

After that, other rock 'n' roll artists came through, one each weekend. Not all were as big as Buddy Holly, but I was there early every time. I didn't really need to show up until after the concerts, but there was no way I was going to miss one.

A month after Buddy's show, Chuck Berry came through. I had the music bug bad by then. I wasn't sure where music was going to take me, but already I knew it was somehow going to take over my life. I and my friends crowded at the back-stage door when Chuck pulled up before the show in a long powder-blue Cadillac that made

our eyes pop. We rushed him, and he glanced over us. We
were a pretty ragtag bunch, but for some reason he settled
on me.

"C'mere, boy."

I approached closer.

"I'll give you five bucks to stick by my car," he said,
pulling out a five. "You don't let no one mess with it.
Awright?"

Me work for Chuck Berry? Hot damn! I could hardly
believe my luck.

So Chuck handed me the five and headed inside. It was
just him and his guitar in its case. No backup band like
Buddy Holly had, no big stage setup. Just Chuck.

I stood proudly by his car for about an hour, soaking up
the glory, but when I heard him start up his show inside —
the crank and whine of the guitar chords through the big
amps — I just couldn't stay outside. I had to get in there. I
gave my cousin Leroy the five bucks to watch the car — kind
of subcontracted the job out — and snuck in and went to
the front of the stage.

Suddenly, halfway through the show, Chuck stopped
between songs and yelled at me, "Hey, kid, what you doin' in
here? You supposed to be with my car."

I'd already become bolder, and I yelled back, "Chuck, you
crazy, man? Me stay out there when you in here?"

Chuck glared at me, but of course he couldn't stop to do
anything about it. He just kept on with his picking and his
duck-walking, and I hung in for the whole show.

Later in life, I met Chuck on several occasions, but I
never really liked him after that first encounter. As an adult,
I could see that he might've been a great rock 'n' roll inno-

vator, but, man, he was mean through and through and one miserable dude to deal with. He served hard time for armed robbery to prove it.

Then one late August day as summer was winding down, Alan Freed brought his rock 'n' roll variety show to the arena, and everything changed for me. Freed was at the peak of his fame in those days with his shows on radio and TV. I knew what Alan was all about. At night, I always tuned in the tinny little AM radio I kept under my pillow to his big rock 'n' roll shows from Cleveland, then from New York.

Freed was later drummed out of the music business and driven to ruin and an early alcoholic death by the so-called Payola Scandal. Alan may have been accepting money from artists and record labels just like everyone else in the business, but the real scandal was that he threw integrated concerts and actually showed black brothers dancing with white girls *right on TV in white folks' living rooms.*

Once again I snuck in early and planted myself on the stage in the wings behind the curtains. I was *right there* as great act after great act came on stage! That afternoon Freed had Frankie Lyman, Dion and the Belmonts, and The Coasters headlining. Man, I was *hooked! This* was my calling. From that moment on, I was going to be a DJ like Allan Freed and hang with all those music stars.

Alan had seen me lurking all afternoon, and when the show ended he walked past, brushing right by me. "Great show, eh, son?" he said.

This time I was so in awe that I bowed and mumbled. I felt like such an idiot. But this wasn't just Freed who'd walked by, this was my *future,* my *inspiration,* and *man* I was excited!

That day I swept up in record time and raced out to catch up with my friends. I was busting to tell them the good news. That I was going to be a "raaaay-dyo" star! I caught up with them. I laid out my heart, my future, my dreams. I was going to be the black Alan Freed. I was going to be a star and hang with music stars.

My little ragtag group was silent for a bit. Finally, my cousin Sonny spoke up. "Nigger, you talkin' like a damn fool. Can't nobody black be no DJ on the ray-dyo."

The remark, casually offered, hit me like a bullet. It hadn't crossed my mind that I could never become a radio star just because I was black. But as the thought sunk in, I realized that Sonny was right. Except for the tiny black soul stations that barely survived on the ends of the dial, relegated to the fringes of radio land, there were no black DJ voices on mainstream radio in North America.

Then I felt anger. Not anger at a corrupt, twisted system. Anger at *myself* for allowing myself to dream so big. To dream so out of line with what society and life had in mind for me. Then those two predators of lost hope — lack of self-confidence and lack of self-esteem — climbed onto my back and began sucking the dream out of me. I could feel my shoulders hunch from their sudden weight. God, how I hated those beasts. Then they crawled right inside and inhabited my body, my mind, my spirit: "Nigger, you dreamin' like a damn fool! Can't no black person be no DJ on the ray-dyo."

I look back now and wonder: why did I listen to Sonny? Why didn't I fight off those predators? But of course the answer is simple: I was only twelve, and weakness within and obstacles in the world beyond hadn't smacked me full in the face before. They did that night for the first time.

I split off from the gang and went off to let my dream die in private, die as it was being born. I believed that night that I'd *never* be a radio man, and I was more depressed and angry than ever. I'd just begun to turn my defeatist attitude around, to dare to dream about *becoming* someone, and I was knocked right back down. Dennis's death years earlier had set in motion a chain of events that had battered my self-esteem and set me up for easy defeat that night.

After the death of my radio dream, I gave up all hope.

Ma and Dad

CHAPTER 2

I don't remember things ever being good for our family as I was growing up.

We had a lot of love in our house but precious little else. We were among the poorest on our block, and even other impoverished black people looked down their noses at the Joneses because we had no tub, no shower, and no hot running water — just cold water, a toilet, and a sink. Our house was a little two-bedroom, wood-frame bungalow at 1096 Mercer Street on Windsor's east side. It wasn't much more than a cottage really, but we sure knew we were in the city because we could look from our front porch and see the smoke stacks and glass towers of Detroit across the river. Much of my extended family lived in Detroit, and it was the city that would most shape my life.

Our house was built in the 1920s by my grandfather, who also built the one next door, where he and my grandma lived. Grandpa Jones worked on the Canadian Pacific

13

Railway as a porter. In the 1920s and 1930s, being a porter was one of the few decent jobs a black man could get, and Grandpa was considered lucky.

One year Dad got it into his head to put a basement under our house, so he had some people start work on it. They lifted the house up three feet with jacks and built a foundation of cinder blocks around the house perimeter, but then Dad ran out of money, and the job was never finished. Everything was just left. So then we had a house sitting up high with a big hole under it and a huge pile of dirt filling up the backyard. Also, the foundation had huge gaps in it where the windows were supposed to go but that only allowed in the wind and the snow, cats gone wild, raccoons, and everything else. It was why our house was so cold in the winter. Water and ice sloshed around in "the basement" and always kept it damp or cold or both.

And the whole house was rotting from the dampness. One time my sister Barb was carrying a heavy pail full of water from the stove, and her foot went right through the dry rot of the kitchen floor. Dad patched the hole, but the entire floor was always threatening to give in.

The one nice thing about the house was a big front porch. And a huge chestnut tree took up the whole front yard, the branches spreading wide and offering some shade. We tied ropes on the branches and played Tarzan for hours, swinging onto the roof. We'd wear a bathing suit or a pair of shorts, take small wooden boards and shape them like knives, and swing away, trying to make that weird half yodel Tarzan used to make — "ah-ee-ah-ah-eeee" — as we swung just like we saw in the movies. We never gave a thought to the fact that Tarzan was white and we were black. As kids, those thoughts never crossed our minds. We didn't know yet that it was an "us and them" world.

Our backyard ran to an alleyway behind the row of houses fronting on Mercer. And every lot had an old shack of some kind near the alley — a garage, a work shed, a woodshed, or a storage shed.

My sister Rosemary and my oldest brother, Leon, lived next door at Grandma Jones's. There was always tension between my grandmother and my ma based on the fact that Dad was thirty-two when he married Mom. He was a high school graduate and fluent in French to boot, while Ma was a sixteen-year-old country girl from North Carolina with less than a grade eight education. Grandma contended it was lust that motivated Dad into the marriage, but in fairness to Dad Ma fibbed to him about her age when they met. Whatever his motivation, he paid for it dearly. The two ladies he cherished the most were in constant conflict.

No two women were more opposite in personality than my mother and my grandmother. Ma was sweet and friendly and loved to laugh, and she accepted people for who they were, while Grandma Jones was aloof and sharp with those who didn't walk the path of righteousness. No matter how much Ma tried to gain Grandma's approval, it never happened. Grandma Jones never gave her her props. I think what really got under Grandma's skin the most was that, at the time of their marriage, Dad was studying to become a minister, but he was forced to put his plans on hold to support a family. But Dad and Ma loved each other very much and were together for forty-four years until the day Dad died in 1977.

In spite of the conflict, I loved living next door to

Grandma Jones, mainly because of Dad's younger sister, Aunt Alta, whom we called Honey because of her sweet nature. Honey loved to cook. She was always baking sweet potato pies, apple upside-down cakes, and soul food dishes — collard greens, pork hocks and beans, southern fried chicken, black-eyed peas and rice. Nobody knew how to bake up a mess of cornbread like she did. You could smell the sweet scent of her cooking two blocks away.

And I knew how to play her for them goodies. I'd fall into her place putting on a long face and faking like I was starving. She'd fall for it every time, and I'd sit at the kitchen table pecking away at all those goodies, telling her how great they tasted. She'd sit next to me with that sweet smile, eating up all my compliments. Yeah, it was cool having Aunt Alta within easy snackin' distance.

But every once in a while, the tension between Ma and Grandma would flare up, mainly when Ma and Dad got into an argument. Dad would beat it next door to Grandma's, and Ma would yell after him, "Go ahead, Mamma's boy." Dad would leave to let things cool down and spill his troubles out to my grandma, and sometimes we kids would sit with Ma and try to comfort her.

Ma always got over her anger quickly, and most of the time she'd walk around humming and singing to herself. She loved to sing old gospel songs and black spirituals. Gospel music always filled our house when I was growing up.

Ma was stocky and short, about four foot eight, with strong forearms from doing the laundry by hand on the scrub board in the same bathtub she scrubbed our carcasses in. And she looked like the original bag lady. She always wore old loose-fitting, thick sweaters, even in the summer, and she always wore hats.

Wherever Ma went, she carried a big handbag that none of us kids could pick up and that even my father found heavy. I got an occasional glimpse inside; it was like a portable curio shop. She'd carry such strange items as books, enough various-sized brushes to go into business, receipts from bills she'd paid years ago, old keys, old letters, framed pictures of her kids and grandkids, old forgotten knitting, and always some money in a knotted hanky. With that handbag, my mother could cause all kinds of chaos in a lineup in a store. She'd get to the cashier, and there'd be people waiting while she fished her hanky out of her bag, and she'd take maybe a full minute just to get the knots untied. And people would wait. Who's going to say anything to an old lady trying to get her money out of a hanky? We kids would try to hurry her along because we'd feel the stares and hear the mutterings, and she'd say, "Hush up, I'm hurryin."

A funny little woman.

Ma was also light skinned, what blacks call "light com-plected." My grandma on her side was white from Winston-Salem, North Carolina, from Dutch heritage, so Ma was biracial. My mother's people were hard-working country folk. It wasn't easy for Ma: to whites, she was black, but to some blacks she was "high yellow," a derogatory term because of her light colouring. Black people were suspicious of whites or anyone who looked even a bit white. Because Ma was light, she took a lot of heat from our darker black neighbours. Blacks do that a lot, call each other names based on skin tone.

Black people call each other many names. Uncle Tom is

the worst, of course — a traitor to your own people. There was a lot of division between the lighter- and darker-skinned blacks in North America at the time, although the situation has improved greatly over the past twenty years.

And Ma was an official mourner. When anybody died in the black communities around Detroit and Windsor, she made it a point to be part of the comforting committee. She had grieving down to an art form. She had the best grieving face I've ever seen: the mournful look; the sad, understanding eyes; and the soft, gentle voice, dripping with condolences: "Be strong, child. They're with the Lord now."

Ma also knew how to stand over a coffin and dish out compliments on how beautiful and peaceful the dearly departed were. I've seen my share of corpses, some those of close friends and loved ones, but I've yet to lay eyes on a good-looking one.

Weird thing was, many of the funerals Ma attended were for either strangers or people she hadn't seen since "Hound Dog" was a hit. And I'm talking not about Elvis's version but about Big Momma Thornton's version *before* Elvis! Didn't matter, though. If Ma got the news there was a stiff to bury, she was there to help send it off to its maker. And don't mention you need someone to sing a eulogy song. Brother, she was on it like icing sugar on apple pie. She'd get up in front of a crowd of people she'd never seen before and belt out her favourite spiritual, "The Last Mile," and her eyes would flutter, she'd toss her head to the heavens, and the whole church would see the whites of her eyes.

Even some of the funerals Ma didn't speak at turned comical. I recall going to a funeral one time with Ma at which a well-known local preacher was eulogizing over some poor fellow we didn't know laid out in his Sunday best. This preacher had that TV evangelical manner, all hype and trumped-up drama. He intoned in a rolling baritone, "Brother Smith was a goooood man."

He paused and waited for a few amens to float up.

"Brother Smith was a riiiiighteous man."

Another pause. A few more amens.

"And Brother Smith is now bound for his reward."

Another scattered chorus of amens.

And then, casting a sharp eye on Brother Smith lying there in the open casket in his fine pinstripe suit jacket with matching vest and trousers, the preacher delivered the clincher. He raised the pitch of his voice and said, "But if Brother Smith thinks he's bound for heaven with that there gold watch and that gold chain, he's got another think comin.'"

The people broke up. They knew that the preacher had had his eye on the watch and chain from the beginning and that they would be staying right here on Earth as "donations."

Dad worked so hard I seldom saw him. During the week, he worked his postal walk from 7 a.m. till 6 p.m. and till noon on Saturdays. After supper, he usually got into serious Bible study during the years he was studying for his pastor's papers. Seemed he was always making notes and looking for scripture to quote. When I was about ten, Dad finally realized his ambition and became an ordained minister of the Baptist Church, and he started his career as a weekend preacher.

Unlike today, the postal service didn't pay much and offered few benefits, so Dad took fill-in preaching assignments around the region for bits of extra money — crumbs, really. He seldom got more than gas money, but he believed that he was doing the Lord's work and that he was working for his reward not so much here in this physical world as in the Great Beyond.

Dad eventually got his own church and congregation in North Buxton, about fifty miles east of Windsor. It's one of the original black settlements in Canada begun in the days of the Underground Railroad, which, of course, wasn't a railroad at all but just a loose network of people helping former slaves flee to the freedom of Canada.

One thing I really admired about Dad was the fact that he practised what he preached. He often preached not to judge others, and he himself *didn't* judge others. Even in later years, when I was running with gangs, messing up, and going to jail, he never judged me, never told me I was going to burn in hell. No matter how much I hurt him, he was always there for me. The day he died, when they lowered his casket into the ground, my heart filled with sorrow and regret for all the hurt and disappointment I'd brought him. How many times had I rejected his invitation to hang together? Those teen years when I'd rather hang on the corners with my boys than be with the father who loved me. When he passed away, he didn't leave anything of worldly value, but he did leave me a gift — the gift of respect. How to treat others.

Part of hanging with Dad was getting our hair cut at Rip's Place. Rip Land lived at the end of our street, in the last house in a line of narrow row houses. Rip lived upstairs, and his shop was one floor below street level, so you walked down narrow concrete steps into the shop. Rip was barber to our whole neighbourhood, and he got his name because of the way he'd rip your hair apart. Bad, baaad barbering. The worst barber on this side of the river. But still, for black folks, old Rip was the only game in town.

And I think Rip invented the proverbial porridge bowl cut. Dad would drag us into Rip's on a Saturday afternoon, and Rip would clamp that bowl on my head, snipping off everything he could see while he talked full speed to Dad, barely noticing the damage he was doing to my hair. Every time I left Rip's place, I knew I was in for a severe teasing until some of my hair grew back.

Still, everyone loved old Rip and gathered at his shop on evenings and weekends. I always loved listening to the fight talk, since boxing was the passion of Rip and all the other grown-ups along the street. Legendary black heavyweight boxing champion Joe Louis — who grew up in Detroit and held the world heavyweight title from 1937 until he retired in 1949 — often came back to Detroit in those days and was just as often the topic of animated barbershop conversations: whom Joe whupped when he was active, whom Joe *could* whup among the current crop of heavyweights. And while they all argued about who was better than whom, I'd dig into dog-eared back issues of the *Ring*, the "Bible of Boxing," and get lost in my own boxing fantasies.

After church work, Dad's other main passion was boxing. When Dad was young, he even won a Michigan State Golden Gloves title. Golden Gloves is the boxing equivalent of amateur hockey or baseball leagues. In 1923, the *Chicago Tribune* sponsored a youth boxing tournament and gave miniature golden gloves to the winners of each age and weight category, which is how it got its name. Many professional champions were Golden Gloves winners in their early years: Sonny Liston, Muhammad Ali, Evander Holyfield, and Mike Tyson, among others.

Back in the 1950s, pro fights were televised three times a week on TV, and I learned about the sweet science watching those early fights at home with Dad. They provided me with a glorious opportunity to witness many of the immortals in their prime: Sugar Ray Robinson, Archie Moore, Jake Lamotta, Rocky Marciano, Kid Gavilan.

On Saturdays, Dad would study his sermon in the afternoon so he could clear the decks to catch his beloved Saturday-night fights. It was a ritual in our household to watch those bouts. Since we had the only TV set in the area, his friends would converge on our house, and for a few hours our small living room sounded like an arena — all kinds of cheering, arguing, and debating going on. It was a contagious atmosphere, and even Ma got in on it, especially when Sugar Ray fought. She'd sit next to Dad and tease him about how fine looking Sugar Ray was. It didn't seem to bother Dad, though, maybe because the Sugar Man was also his favourite.

Years later, in 1962, when I was fifteen, I had the honour of meeting Sugar Ray at the Motor City Gym in Detroit. By then, he was pushing forty, but he could still dance. I happened to be in the gym training for my first Golden Gloves tournament — in the novice division — when we heard this commotion. I turned around to check it out, and not more than ten feet from me was the Sugar Man in person! He was in town to promote an upcoming fight at the Olympia.

Near the end of his training session, Sugar Ray saw me hanging off the apron of the ring, clearly fascinated with everything he did, and, to my surprise, he beckoned me into the ring. I froze for a second. This was the patron saint of pugilism, and he was inviting a young 130-pound novice into the ring? I blundered through a couple of two-minute rounds, and he just played with me, basically gave me free pointers. It was an awesome experience. Worked too. I won a novice lightweight Golden Gloves title for the Windsor area later that year. It would be the first of many Golden Gloves titles I'd win over the next twenty years.

After we finished training, Sugar Ray laid that sweet smile on me and told me boxing was cool, but education was far more important. He asked me if I was still in school. I lied and said I was, but by that time, by age fifteen, I was skipping school with more regularity than he was skipping rope.

Hey, Buckwheat!

CHAPTER 3

I didn't really know what racism was until I hit the school system.

In September 1954, I started kindergarten at Prince Edward Public School. On my first day, I was pumped at the prospect of making new friends and discovering the world beyond our small house and our sad-sack neighbourhood. There had to be a big, wonderful world out there, and I was eager to see it. Also, it would get me out of our house to a place that was warm and bright and clean.

Until my first day of kindergarten, the only schoolroom I'd experienced was Bible class at Dad's church. Never did feel out of place there, probably because all the other kids in Bible class were also black. We learned about love and compassion, about the Good Samaritan and Moses, how God saw all people as equals. We never heard ugly words like "nigger," "shine," "spook," or "coon."

But in kindergarten, everything felt different. For a start, being the only black kid in my class set me apart from the others, and I could sense it from day one by the peculiar way they stared at me. It made me feel out of place. All the people I'd seen on TV to that point were white, and they were my heroes: the Lone Ranger, Roy Rogers, Gene Autry. When I went into my childhood fantasy world with my heroes — all whites — I always fit right in, galloping across the range on Silver, or on Trigger, with Dale Evans and Pat Brady tagging along. My blackness never bothered anyone in my flights of fantasy, though I did wonder sometimes where the black good guys were. How come they never showed up? The only blacks I saw on TV or heard on the radio were silly characters: Rochester with Jack Benny, Amos and Andy, and black savages Tarzan was always beating up on. Not exactly hero figures.

The Little Rascals was another popular TV series of the day, and most kids watched it faithfully. The series featured a couple of bulgy-eyed, foot-shuffling, self-effacing black kids called Stymie and Buckwheat. White kids may have found them comical, but they sure didn't do us black kids any good. In school, kids got on me every chance they got. "Hey, Buckwheat," or "Stymie," they'd holler. I'd pretend it didn't bother me. I'd laugh along with the other kids, but underneath I felt a deep sense of humiliation.

Suddenly, my blackness *mattered*. It made me *different*. It gave the other kids something to ridicule, though I couldn't figure out why they'd want to. What had I done? I was nice to everybody. I was respectful, polite, soft spoken, even shy. Eventually, I learned that these positive attributes were the exact opposite of what I'd need to survive in the world beyond our home and my childhood fantasies.

One morning, while the teacher had stepped out of the classroom, my longtime tormentor Red Turner came over and told me to get off the fire engine I was playing on. I just kept playing and making siren noises, so he gave me a push that sent me flying to the floor. I pushed him back and climbed back on. He jumped up, called me a nigger, and punched me so hard in the face that he knocked me clean off the fire engine again. Before I could get to my feet, he pounced on me and began flailing away with both hands. He got one punch through that landed on my nose, and blood began to gush onto my new white T-shirt.

In those few seconds, I learned that, even when you're minding your own business, there's always somebody who wants to hurt you. That day the game changed for me. I stopped trusting the other kids. At any hint of animosity, I took off.

After that beating, I became the class recluse. I stuck to myself. I also began to notice classmates staring at me more. When I caught their eyes, they'd quickly turn away, but I got to know what a certain stare stood for. Some looks were out of curiosity, others just out of pity: that poor soul, it's not his fault he's black. Many blacks felt so inferior we even attempted to change our appearance and picked up on various white behaviours. I tried to walk, talk, dress, and act like I was white, which led me to be even more confused.

About four months into kindergarten, I was promoted to grade one, apparently because I was too bright for kindergarten. The truth is I could read better than most kids my age at that time because my older sister Barbara had spent so much time reading to me and helping me with words before I'd even hit school. She was a year older than I was, and I idolized her, followed her everywhere. Everyone thought it great that I was moved ahead, and it was a real ego booster. But the move only ended up causing me trouble because, while I was advanced at reading in those early days, I had trouble with math, and then my reading began to fall behind as I withdrew. Soon I began to have trouble with school generally. The move also meant I was now exposed full time to Red Turner, also in grade one. All in all, the move forward was a mistake.

During those years, I spent a lot of weekends at my Aunt Ida's in Detroit. Aunt Ida lived in the Brewster Projects, in those days considered one of the toughest 'hoods in America. Many of the kids carried knives and straight razors, and some of the older ones had guns.

When I was there, I was dogged a lot about my Canadian accent. "Man, you talk like a white boy!" they'd laugh. Or "Man, why you be soundin' like a honky-talkin' nigger?" To dodge their ridicule, I had to learn fast how to walk the walk and talk the talk like a Detroit kid. It wasn't too difficult to pick up the talk because most of the dialect Detroit blacks used originated in the South, and my mother's people being from North Carolina I'd heard it a lot. Before long, I was acting like a Motor City brother with the moves and the jive: "What's shakin', baby? Ain't nuthin' to it but to do it."

Just when I had the American accent and strut down pat, it was time to cross the border back into the Great White North. Come Monday morning, I was back at school trying to fit into the white culture again. I learned to switch styles very quickly depending on the situation, but in truth I suffered from a severe identity crisis. Blacks thought I acted white, and whites thought I acted black, a heavy trip to lay on a kid who'd never even been schooled in his own culture. I wasn't sure *what* I should be.

Unbelievably, one of our schoolbooks was *The Adventures of Little Black Sambo*, a story about a nappy-headed, thick-lipped black kid who lived in the African jungles with his mother, Black Mambo, and his father, Black Jumbo. To me, the book was an insensitive piece of demeaning trash. It was humiliating! The teacher would be reading *Black Sambo*, and the class was full of white kids, and I was the only black child in the room, and in the background I'd hear the snickers and catch the glances in my direction. It made me a laughing stock! The *Black Sambo* material was part of the education system that cultivated the minds of our future leaders. Little wonder racism still plays a major role in much of today's society. Many of our decision makers and leaders are remnants of those times.

As the school year progressed, Red Turner and his hostile glares kept me in a state of constant anxiety. He hassled me at recess, at lunch, and after school. If I ran into him on the street, in the store, in the schoolyard, or at the movies, he was on me. I was too fragile and too polite to know what to do about it, and I was too frightened to tell anybody to get it to stop. Today I'm sensitive toward victims of bullies because I've lived through the fear and misery of being beaten and intimidated. I know how bullies steal your self-esteem and make you feel helpless.

Turner's bullying would dog me for many years, and when I finally got Red off my back it ruined my chances at school and started my career as a street punk and thief.

The Angel of Death

CHAPTER 4

Things really started to go bad for me at school after Dennis died.

The closest I'd been to death before then was when my grandfather died the year before. He was in an open casket until burial in North Buxton. The day before the funeral, we drove to the town, and that night we kids were piled into beds in the upstairs of the parsonage, next door to the church. The room was warmed by heat from the potbellied stove downstairs drifting up to the second floor through a wooden grate in the floor. In the middle of the night, I woke up and rolled over, and, because the grate was next to my cot, I was drawn to look down, and there, right below me in a soft glow of light and in a plain wooden casket, was Granddad.

He was flat on his back, eyes closed, hands folded across his chest and resting at his throat. He looked so strange. Real but not real. He was there, yet he wasn't there. He was *dead.*

31

I wanted to turn away, but I couldn't stop staring. I was both fascinated and terrified. The sight of Granddad's lifeless body spooked me. I couldn't sleep the rest of the night with a dead body right below me because I knew that the Angel of Death had come to claim Granddad when he'd died, and I was afraid that the angel might come back to visit him again before he was buried. The Angel of Death would become a problem for me for many years.

At Dennis's funeral, my mother set pictures of Dennis inside the small, open casket. I was struck by how peacefully he was lying there, dressed in a knitted sleeper. Like Grandpa, he looked like he was sleeping, not gone. For many years afterward, Ma kept the pictures in a cupboard. Sometimes, when she thought nobody was around, she'd take them out and stare at them. She missed him something awful. I'd also be drawn to look at them. I'd take them out and stare at them, fascinated and confused. That was my little brother, someone I loved and was *attached* to, a part of my life, of our family. Gone now. To where? What *was* death anyway? Was Dennis really in heaven? What *was* heaven? Would he ever come back for a visit? It felt strange to be so close to that powerful and mysterious process everyone called death. And all the things my parents kept telling me didn't add up to someone going to paradise. Even being so young, I was able to rationalize that something horrible had transpired, and no matter how many euphemisms they used to disguise death I wasn't buying in.

Years later, in therapy as an adult, I learned that I refused to believe that Dennis had really died. I believed that he had just been sleeping when they'd put him in the ground and that maybe one day he would return to us.

I began to live in a constant state of fear of the angel, especially after the lights went out. Hours before bedtime, scary feelings would overcome me. The thought of going into that room where Dennis had been taken by the angel filled me with trepidation. So much so that I'd offer to do things that were unnatural for kids, like volunteering to wash dishes, sweep floors, and empty the garbage. Ma, worn out from dealing with us kids and other countless chores, was quick to take me up on the offers. Still, stalling only prolonged my agony. Eventually, Ma would send me off to bed and always with a stern warning: "Boy, Lord have mercy on your behind in the morning if you wet the bed tonight!" Ma wasn't blowing smoke either. She meant it!

My fear of the night in those years came, strangely, from strong Southern Baptist hell-and-brimstone beliefs all around me, not only in the church that I attended every week, but also in our home. Religious grown-ups around me had so many scary names for death — the Angel of Death, the Grim Reaper and his Harvest of Dead Souls, Lucifer, many others — and Ma and Dad would say things like "If you ain't good, boy, the Devil's gonna come and git you" or "The Lord sees all. You can't hide *anything* from him." If it weren't the Devil, then it might be the Lord's messenger, Gabriel, who came for you. Whenever you did something wrong, you were going, by *somebody's* hand, straight to hell, where we all knew you burned for eternity no matter who took you there. Sometimes I wondered if the Lord and the Devil ever cooperated on snatching souls and then decided later who got to keep them.

And all those Baptists would say, ominously, "No one knows when the end days are near, but when the Lord comes he will come *like a thief in the night.*" That phrase reverberated in my young mind: *like — a — thief — in — the — night.* I got the message: all bad things are going to happen at night, when it's dark.

It had been so for Dennis.

I sometimes wondered what a little eighteen-month-old baby could have done to warrant such an extreme action. But if little Dennis could incur God's wrath, then it was certain that I was incurring it almost every waking hour of my life.

And so the nightmares began.

In them, an old man dressed in black — the same kind of guy who'd come for Dennis — worked with the angel and would snatch me out of bed and fling me into a scuffed leather carrying case — the same kind Dennis had been tossed into. Then he'd cart me to the morgue and dump me into a coffin and shut the lid. I'd be lying in the blackness of the coffin, screaming, begging someone to rescue me. I was buried alive. In my mind, the evil man who'd taken my brother's body was out there in the shadows of the house, waiting to get his cold fingers on my throat. Waiting to squeeze the life out of me too.

Our bedroom was so small that only one double bed fit into it, leaving a small space to walk in. So we slept six to one bed, what we called "3 toes up and 3 toes down," which meant two with our heads at the top of the bed and two with our heads at the bottom, four of us lying side by side like sardines in a can. We bathed only once a week — the rest of the time we just sponged down — and we'd wear beat-up running shoes almost all year, so you'd wake up in the middle of the night from an inadvertent kick and find a pair of stinking, crusty feet in your face. We thought everyone slept like that.

Our sleep was fretful at the best of times, but my brothers and sisters didn't seem to be bothered by the angel like I was. I was the one who stayed awake night after night. I gave up telling my mother and father about my problem because the couple of times I did try to tell them they said that I was imagining things, that I should just close my eyes and go to sleep.

Our house was too small to have closets or room for dressers, so many of our clothes hung about the house on hangers hooked onto the tops of doors or doorframes. When the air stirred the clothes, I'd see a movement — a shadow here, a ripple there — and I'd stop breathing to listen. I'd see shadows I couldn't place and hear sounds I couldn't explain. My bladder might have been busting — I might have had to go pee in an awful way — but I'd lie rigid as a board, terrified to move, afraid to walk through the terror of the living room to the bathroom. I knew that the angel was prowling around our house waiting for me. If I had to pee myself, I was going to do it *right there*, in bed. I wasn't getting up for *anything*.

Many nights I couldn't hold it. I could feel it coming, and I'd scrunch up my face and let go, and I'd feel hot urine running all over my pyjamas and then the sheets and mattress. I'd soak myself and feel it turn quickly from warm to cold. Then there'd be a mad scramble by my brothers and sisters for a dry spot on the bed, but I'd be too terrified to move and would then lie in a cold, soaked bed, still watching, still listening. As dawn brought light to our room, I would still be awake, exhausted from a night without sleep, but at least

I'd evaded the angel one more night.

My brothers were bed wetters too but not every night like me. You'd hear somebody stirring in the middle of the night — first you'd hear a stretch and a yawn and then an "ahhhhh," and then it would sound like a tap going off. That'd be one of my brothers. Piss all over you. In later years, I used to say that the Jones family had invented the first water bed, but we never made a nickel from it. I learned years later that it may have been a gene in our family, though it was a common thing with many of the young brothers in our area.

My bed-wetting caused much tension between my parents and me. I knew that Ma was going to whip me in the morning when she found out that I had wet the bed again. She had a saying: "I'm gonna whip your bottom till times get better." Trouble was times never got better for us. And when my mother whipped my bottom, she whipped my *bare* bottom. She pulled my underwear down and gave me five or six whacks with a belt that brought up dark welts. Even going for a clean change of underwear meant a whipping because it was a tip-off that I had wet underwear, so I was going to school with the same urine-stained underwear three or four days in a row.

To avoid Ma's wrath, I'd get up fast, pull on my jeans, run out the door, and be gone before eight. I'd say I had to get to school early. I knew that this tactic would only raise her suspicions and that Ma would go straight to my room and smell the reason for my flight, but at least I was alive. I'd do *anything* to avoid having the breath squeezed out of me in the middle of the night.

Also, living in a home where kids constantly piss the bed

leaves the stench of stale urine lingering in the air. It gets
into your clothes, into your furniture, on your skin, and in
your hair. The offensive odour made me the brunt of many
jokes. Seemed like everybody in the damn city was hip to
our house's stinky reputation! Kids taunted me about my
smelly clothes and house. Being frail and sickly, I couldn't do
much about it, so I kept the anger and hurt bottled up.

But it wasn't just the angel that terrified me in my bed. It
was also the rats.

Sewer Rats

Unlike the Angel of Death, who was sneaky and stealthy, the rats I could hear clearly. I'd hear them scurrying across the hardwood, scratching inside the walls, foraging in the kitchen, rattling cans in the garbage.

They seemed to get worse after Dennis died. Maybe it was the extreme cold of that winter that forced them inside more often at night. They'd waddle their bloated carcasses down from the Peerless Dairy, located at the end of the block, about fifteen houses away from ours. As well as trucks, horse-drawn wagons were still being used at the dairy, and the big stables attracted mice and rats. Also, all the dairy products — milk, cream, butter, ice cream, which we were always trying to find a way to swipe, especially ice-cream bars — were made on site and, of course, attracted not only ordinary mice and rats but also fat sewer rats — those that lived and bred in the network of sewers along our street.

A sewer rat isn't like an ordinary rat. Some could be fifteen inches long, larger than any squirrel. And they have big ugly whiskers and rows of big ugly teeth, which carried every kind of disease. Everyone said it was rats that had spread the Black Death in the Middle Ages, and we were always afraid of being bitten by one and catching some disease. The creamery was crawling with them. They were so common that people used to shoot them for target practice in the evening. A man we knew who lived next to the dairy used to sit outside in the evening with his .22 and pick them off for sport.

A colony of them made a nest in the muck under our house where the basement should have been, and they'd squeeze their greasy hides through holes in our kitchen floor in search of food. You could hear them at night. They were so active and so loud they'd often wake us.

We had to put everything away every night. Even then they'd get inside, looking for anything. They'd scavenge for table scraps, for garbage. They'd come in where they smelled even a *trace* of food. There was always something the rats could get at, and they knew it. Our house was high on their shopping list.

One night I heard the rats *and* the Angel of Death.

The angel was in our house. I just knew it. He was in our kitchen, and I knew he had come for me. I could hear him. He was making a kind of hollow, scraping sound. I lay awake petrified for hours listening to him. But in the morning, Ma said that it was only the rats that had turned over the garbage and spread cans around the kitchen, rolling them around all night, trying to reach down to the food still stuck to the insides. She said she'd heard them but hadn't had the energy to get up and fight them.

But Barbara fought them all the time. She was a tough girl, and I believe she actually enjoyed fighting the rats because she saw them as filthy invaders of our home. When she got up in the middle of the night to go to the bathroom, she took a broken broom handle with her, ready to do battle, and sometimes I followed her. Those were the few occasions when I managed to get through the night without wetting the bed.

Our kitchen had only one light hanging from the ceiling in the middle of the room. A piece of cord dangled from the light, and you had to reach up and pull it for the light to come on. I was too short to reach it, but Barbara, being a little taller, just managed to reach it. Most of the time, when the rats heard us approaching, they'd scurry for cover. But sometimes they'd be so wrapped up in what they were doing they'd just plain ignore our presence. Barbara would turn on the light, and I'd peek around her, and sometimes we'd catch one right up on the kitchen table, maybe licking bits of butter or some crumbs, and it wouldn't skitter — it would turn and hiss and spit. It was scary.

One night, before we had even turned in, we caught a huge one on the table that was so engrossed in eating that it didn't hear us. Barb crept up behind it and took a mighty swipe with the broom handle. The rat jumped onto the floor and ran for its hole, but before it could get there she cut it off, and it bared its teeth and sprang up at her. She swung at it again, and it sprang back up at her. A full-blown fight broke out, with Barb swinging and the rat jumping up. It scared the hell out of me. She must have clubbed it about five times before it finally stayed down, stunned if not dead.

It was a vicious fight, and I was hiding behind her, but she was having a great battle. She then smashed that rat over and over until she killed it for sure, and its dark rat blood was all over the floor. Then she shoved its limp carcass across the linoleum, and its body made a reddish-black streak on the floor all the way to the hole where it had come from.

I recall another incident. In our kitchen was a massive, cast-iron woodstove with four large circular cooking surfaces covered with heavy iron lids that you could lift by inserting a special iron handle into a groove. Above were steel shelves for storing pots and pans. One night the family was in the living room watching TV, and Barb decided to hit the kitchen to make some peanut butter sandwiches. I followed her out. Ma had been heating a large pail of water on the stove for our Saturday-night baths, and, as we were passing the stove, I spotted a large rat on the upper shelf sniffing around. I jumped behind Barb, and she grabbed a broom and began jabbing at the rat and forcing it to back up as far on the shelf as possible. It was cornered, so in desperation it attempted to leap to the floor. Instead, it fell into the pail of water.

The water hadn't reached a full boil, but it was still pretty hot, and the rat was trapped, with no escape. It desperately began swimming around, scratching to try to get up the sides of the huge pot, when Barb grabbed the lid and slammed it on the pot. We could hear the rat thrashing and squealing in agony inside as the water temperature rose, and it was eventually boiled alive. It may sound cruel and sadistic, but I had no pity for that rat. It could have died a thousand deaths, and it wouldn't have bothered me a bit. The rats had been tormenting and terrorizing me for years. As far as I was concerned, this was one less rat to worry about.

Dad also took the rat raids personally and tried every method available to rid our house of the vermin. Rat poison worked to some degree. Problem was they'd crawl under the house or into the walls and die, and for weeks our house would be filled with the stench of their rotting corpses. Dad used traps and even got a big tomcat, but nothing seemed to work completely.

Finally, Dad had enough of the rats, and he brought home this sorry-looking grey mutt about the size of a large cat. One of his mail route people had given it to him as a gift. It had a muscular build with strong shoulders and a thick, powerful neck. Dad told us it was called a rat terrier, bred to hunt and kill rats. From day one, that dog lived up to its name. That very evening it made its first kill.

Rosemary and I were playing with the mutt on the front room sofa when Dad came creeping into the room with his finger to his lips. "Quiet," he whispered. He scooped up the mutt and crept toward the kitchen with it, but the rat spotted him and darted into the bathroom. Dad rushed across the kitchen, tossed the mutt into the bathroom, then slammed the door behind it. The entire family gathered in the kitchen to witness the event. For a peace-loving man, my dad hated those rats as much as any of us did. We could hear one hell of a scuffle going on inside the bathroom — crashing, snarling, banging, yelping, hissing — until finally the dog came out carrying the limp body of that filthy, bloody rat in its jaws. Dad took the rat from him and threw it outside into the farthest corner of the backyard.

Sometimes Dad would send the mutt under the house, and we'd hear this hellish scuffle, and the mutt would come out proudly carrying a dead rat. The rats must have gotten the message, because after a few months we scarcely saw any around the house. We had won!

But even minus the rats, I still wasn't about to go through that kitchen at night. I was still afraid of the Angel of Death and pissed the bed for years to come.

CHAPTER 6

Getting Clean for the Lord

Being the son of a preacher man meant that church played a major role during my early years. Even if Dad was dog tired from his mail delivery work all week, on Wednesday evenings and on Sundays we had to be in church — unless we were critically ill. I spent some serious time in the Lord's house.

Sunday was church day — all day. It began with Sunday school, then church, then church again at night. So Sunday mornings we got up early to a quick breakfast, usually of puffed wheat. Ma would bring out the big glass milk pitcher from the icebox, but real milk was a rare luxury, so what we usually had was powdered milk that she barely had time to mix, so the insides of our glasses would be covered with sticky white goo, and, when Ma poured, big lumps of white mush would plop into our glasses and bowls. I hated that stuff. It tasted like watered-down chalk grindings.

But before Sunday morning came Saturday night — bath night. "We gotta get clean for the Lord," Ma would say.

Getting clean meant taking turns getting scrubbed down by Ma in the huge galvanized tin bathtub, which she kept stored in a corner of the kitchen. She'd haul it to the middle of the kitchen floor, boil water in the big pot, and dump nearly boiling water in with freezing cold water, so what we ended up with was lukewarm water that soon went cool and then outright cold.

One at a time, alone in the kitchen with Ma, we'd strip down and hop into the same water that those before us had used and those after us would get, and she'd scrub us down. And, boy, was she rough! She was all business with that old thick-bristled scrub brush, doing the Lord's work to get us clean. Many a time I thought she was going to scrape the nuts right off me. She'd soak us all over with a big ladle, dipping it in the dirty, soapy water and dumping it on our heads, and we'd get water and soap in our eyes. It would sting like hell. I'd scream out "Ma!" She'd just say, "Oh, hush up. You gotta get clean. We're gonna see the Lord tomorrow."

She scrubbed my father last, and we used to peek through the keyhole and watch. We couldn't help giggling, and Dad would hear us and yell, "Hey, what're you kids doing there?" We'd scatter. We were supposed to be in bed.

After breakfast on Sunday morning, it was out to my dad's old '46 Ford sedan. The whole family would pile in, and off we'd go. I don't think there was ever a Sunday that we didn't have to stop at least once on the way there. The smell of gas was always so strong in that old car, and one of us always got car-sick.

Dad was one of those two-fisted drivers, gripping the steering wheel with both hands till his knuckles turned white while looking straight ahead. And he drove *s-o-o-o-o*

slooooowly. Everybody passed us in a big hurry, but the only
things we ever passed were the white lines on the highway.

But we always had a lot of fun on Sundays, and I loved
going. It was our big day out. Dad's church in North Buxton
was a little one-room wood building beside the railway
tracks in the north end of town. Although it was a mixed
community, his church was known as a black church, mostly
for area black farm families. Most of the time the church was
half full, which, on a good Sunday, meant about fifty people
— farmers and their wives and their kids. These people
came in their old seersucker suits and their old clothes,
humble, salt-of-the-earth farm people. Often they came in
their coveralls right out of the fields — some so bent over
and tired that they could hardly walk but coming to give
thanks to the Lord.

For us kids, Sunday school at about ten o'clock was followed at eleven by the church service. While we were in
Sunday school, Dad would prepare his sermon. My father
was a good speaker but not the hell-and-brimstone type. He
spoke his message quietly, calmly, not like some of the others
— like Ma, for instance, who got emotional and stirred up
when they sermonized. And Dad always prepared his sermons in detail, often scanning newspapers or magazines for
issues to share with his congregation.

Dad often sang as part of his service. He sang one song
so often I knew every pause and tremolo, but I always loved
to hear it: "How Great Thou Art." Sometimes Ma would get
up and sing a duet with him of "Peace in the Valley." She
would be up front dancing and clapping and hollering
amen! Sometimes, when she was up on the podium singing
with Dad, it was tough to keep a straight face, especially

when she matched his high notes. Her eyes rolled back into her head. Looked like she was having a fit. It was a hilarious sight. But we dared not laugh, 'cause if we did we were in big trouble! Ma had zero tolerance for acting a fool in church.

On one Easter Sunday, though, Ma was singing "The Old Rugged Cross" to a full house. Suddenly, she flung her head back and hit a high note, and her eyes got to fluttering, and then they rolled so far back into her head we saw nothing but the whites. Man, forget it! We kids all broke up in a chorus of laughter. I swear everybody in the church looked at us, and Ma shot us one of those steely *I'm-gonna-whip-your-behinds-but-good!* looks.

A few seconds later, she hit another high note. Back went her head again, she looked upward to the heavens, and her eyelids got to fluttering again. Then her eyeballs disappeared completely. Leroy jabbed me and snickered, and I lost it. I got to laughing so hard my insides hurt.

The next couple of minutes were sweating-it-out time. I sat there trying to look as innocent as possible. Hoping Ma would forget. Never happened! After she finished her solo, she bowed to the congregation, excused herself, walked down off the stage, snatched me up by the arm, dragged me behind the church, and wore my ass out! I heard my father inside the church shouting out one of his Bible quotes: "Do *not* spare the rod and spoil the child!" I also heard a whole lot of amens in support of that quote.

Fewer than twenty yards from the church, the train passed by, sometimes two or three times during a service. Everything inside would shake and rattle: the windows, the walls, the lights, the pulpit — *everything*. My father would halt the service for a few minutes with a patient smile on his face and wait until the train had passed; then he'd just pick up and carry on where he'd left off.

I recall that Dad always began his sermons with the words *kind friends*. That opening always struck me: these people *were* kind, and they *were* our friends, and Dad had helped to make them both of those things.

After the service was the part I loved the most because we'd always get invited somewhere for the afternoon until the six o'clock evening service. Because my father's people were from North Buxton, we had a lot of relatives there, so we always had someone inviting us over — cousins, aunts, uncles, friends of the family. And because they all lived on farms, I'd get a chance to run around outdoors and chase cows and pigs. As a city kid, I loved it. And these people always ate so well. They had big kitchen tables filled with things grown on the farm: potatoes, ham, beans, sweet potato pie, hot biscuits, gravy, and chicken southern fried the way only black people can make it.

The biggest thrill of the day for me was riding a huge Clydesdale named Clyde. He was a massive, magnificent-looking dark brown creature. Real gentle too. We'd take turns riding him up and down the path from the house to the barn. Never seen a tamer, gentler giant than Clyde. And he was also a big mooch. We'd be sitting at the kitchen table eating, and Clyde would come strutting right up to the open window, pop his massive head in, and beg for a treat, so we'd lay an apple or a few lumps of sugar on him.

And I remember bringing the cows in from the pasture before the evening service as I ran along with one of my uncles. They were some of the best moments of my life; the peace and tranquillity of those carefree warm summer afternoons were so far from the bad vibes of the city.

One thing I always wondered about was why church was called the Lord's house. I thought the Lord must have been one rich dude to own so many homes. In every church we visited, I'd hear someone say we were in the Lord's house. But I thought it was weird that the Lord never showed up considering he owned all these houses. In fact, if it weren't for the large portrait that hung on the wall behind the pulpit of our church and the one above my grandma's living room sofa, I'd never have had a clue what he looked like. I knew by these pictures he was a white man with shoulder-length hair and a beard, but it didn't matter to me what colour he was.

I also wondered why my folks called Jesus the Lord. He wasn't the same man in the photos with the flowing robes; Jesus was the man on the cross with only a loincloth. So why did they always bow their heads and drop to their knees when they talked to him? Besides being confusing, this puzzle consumed me with curiosity. I wanted some answers! But it seemed like every time I asked people about why they were praying to this invisible person I got the brush-off.

"We live by faith," Ma would say.

"What's faith?" I'd ask.

"You'll understand someday."

I thought the answers were lame. They did nothing to satisfy my curiosity.

One afternoon when I was about seven, my curiosity got the best of me. My father was the guest speaker at a church in Detroit, and about halfway through his message he began to speak about what a blessing it was that day to be in that wonderful house of the Lord. That's when it hit me! "Hey! Maybe the Lord's here today." I began to search among the congregation for a white face. I checked out every face in the place, and not one was white. Finally, out of frustration, I asked Ma to point the Lord out to me.

"Honey," she answered, "you can't see him, but he's here."

"Where?"

"In spirit."

"How do you know he's here if you can't see him?"

"You can feel his presence all around us. Now hush up!"

But I was still confused.

"Does he live right in this here church?"

"No, honey," she said, "he lives up in heaven with God."

That really charged me up! Wasn't heaven the place where Dennis moved to? Man! I had to meet the Lord and find out more about that place!

"Ma, you sure the Lord is here?" I asked.

"Oh yes, baby," she smiled and nodded, "he's right here with us." She patted me on the knee. "Now be still!"

After the service, when everybody retired to the basement area to eat, I crept back upstairs and felt around in the air, trying to touch this invisible Lord. I whispered his name and asked about Dennis. I wanted to know if my baby brother was really up there, but I didn't hear a peep out of the Lord that afternoon.

Meanwhile, my bed-wetting continued to haunt me.

Most mornings I was still pulling my jeans on right over my wet underwear. It's impossible to mask the stench of dried urine, but I attempted to do so by splashing some of my father's Old Spice aftershave lotion on my jeans, but it only amplified the stench.

At school, the kids were constantly poking fun at me. They called me names like funky fool and stinky Chuck. Being the brunt of degrading remarks goes to your heart, to your soul, to your psyche. It attacks your self-esteem and makes you feel inferior. I'd sit there stinking and dying inside. I stank up not only our whole house but my school classroom too. When we shared schoolbooks, nobody wanted to sit with me because I stank like hell.

One time our teacher was moving up and down the aisles reading when suddenly, in the middle of a sentence, she stopped and inquired, "What's that awful smell?" My classmates knew it was me, and they all turned to look at me as the teacher tried to pinpoint the smell. She finally stopped near my desk. Every eye in the room was on me.

"It's Jones!" yelled Red Turner. "He always stinks!"

The class burst into laughter, but I was so ashamed I wanted to die on the spot.

"Charles, is that awful smell you?"

I started to cry, but she was very nice. She said, "Let's go down and see the nurse."

The nurse cleaned me up, which I really appreciated. I was in awful shape, all chapped from wearing urine-soaked underwear all the time. She sponged me all around my privates, where there was an ugly red rash, though today you'd probably get arrested for helping a little kid like that. She put some cream on and said she was going to have a talk with my mother. She did. She called Ma in for a talk, but it didn't change anything.

My mother didn't know about the rash, but I don't blame

her, because I did everything I could to hide it from her. All she knew was that she was tired of us pissing the bed and her and Dad having to buy a new mattress every few months. My mattresses got so bad that you could get stuck in the middle of the bed, where the mattress had rotted through from the urine and the springs stuck out to catch you. My mother would take a piece of cardboard and lay it across the bed to guard us from the springs and then lay a rubber sheet over that, but in the middle of the night the rubber sheet would get moved around, and when we pissed the cardboard and then the mattress would just get soaked again. So every five or six months Dad had to buy a new mattress.

And while I'd heard the word *nigger* on occasion while growing up, I was really coming to understand its ugly meaning now. Kids would mutter, "Hey, you stink, nigger." And "Get away from me, nigger, you stink." And I noticed that, anytime I got into a talk or an argument or a fight with a white kid, the first thing to come out was "nigger." When I heard the word on street corners in our neighbourhood, it was always said sort of affectionately. You'd hear the older blacks joking with each other: "Aw, nigger, you ain't this . . . " and "Aw, nigger, you ain't that. . . . " But in school, it was different. It was meant to hurt and be a put-down. And I heard it all the time — in the classroom, on the way to school, in the playground, after school.

So my alienation worsened.

Also, when you're six, seven, eight years old, everyone teases you about having a girlfriend or a boyfriend, but I never had a girlfriend. No little girl would have wanted to be known as my girlfriend. One girl, Susan Kish, got a crush on me, and everyone started treating her like she was some kind of weirdo because of it.

So I started to sit alone.

I could feel that, by about grade three, I was beginning to go into a shell. I'd sit at the back of the class, away from the other kids, so they couldn't smell me. While the others were studying, I was lost in my own daydream world, where I closed everybody out. I knew I was losing it. But by grade three, I didn't give a damn anymore.

CHAPTER 7

The Lunch Bag Bandit

I stopped keeping up at school because the nightmares that continued to haunt me kept me awake most nights, and by morning I couldn't think straight. Often I was so tired I'd fall asleep in class, which put me in bad with my teachers. They'd send home notes to my parents, who in turn got uptight with me. Ma dealt with the problem by sending me to bed an hour earlier, which only meant that I had an hour longer to deal with the dark. Next morning I'd be back in school fighting sleep and losing the battle again.

My personality changed from happy and outgoing to short tempered. I was growing more angry and frustrated with each passing day. I felt like there was a bomb inside me with the wick slowly burning down. My self-esteem was dropping fast. About that time, I also became a thief, which surprised me at first, but I took to it quickly and with a vengeance that felt good. It felt like a way of striking back. It also led to one of my most humiliating school experiences

— the first time I was strapped in front of the class.

It came about because, to avoid Ma's whippings, I used to leave the house in such a hurry that I didn't even take the time to grab a quick breakfast or take a lunch. So, by the time I reached school, my stomach was growling with hunger pangs. I never went home for lunch, which meant I had to last the entire day without food.

There were days when my hunger was so intense that I got sick. Those long, hungry days put me in a desperate situation. I had to discover a way to resolve the problem or continue to suffer. One morning, just as I was about to enter the classroom, I spotted a kid named Lonnie placing his lunch in his locker. In that moment, a larcenous idea came to me. Until then, I'd never stolen a thing, but I was determined that I was going to steal Lonnie's lunch.

I followed Lonnie into class and took my place at my desk. I waited until I was certain that the hallways were clear and that all the kids were in class, and then I got the teacher's permission to go to the washroom. I headed in that direction, casing out the halls along the way, and, when I was positive it was all clear, I rushed back, quickly opened Lonnie's locker, snatched his lunch, and raced full speed to the boys' washroom. In heart-pounding seconds, I was crouched in a stall wolfing down a meatloaf sandwich and a large slice of delicious chocolate cake.

During the entire ordeal, my body shook with fear. But I also felt a bizarre new sensation: satisfaction. Stealing Lonnie's lunch charged me up, gave me a feeling of pride. It was like I'd just pulled off a big heist. Better still, I'd discovered the solution to my hunger problem. It made me feel independent. I thought, "I don't have to depend on Ma or anybody else to feed me anymore."

After that, I scouted the halls every morning in search of a new victim. Generally, I zeroed in on the ones who were dressed the best. I figured they'd have the best food. After a few weeks, I became so proficient at stealing lunches that I began to grow cocky and careless. Word had been circulating around school with regard to lunches being swiped, and the kids even had a nickname for the thief, the Lunch Bag Bandit. The name amused me, made me laugh. I felt like Zorro, and like him I thought I'd never get caught.

Late one morning, about the third week of my lunch bag crime spree, I targeted a victim whose locker was located on the second floor near the south end of the school. It was my most risky challenge so far. Until then, I'd restricted my activities to the first floor. About ten-thirty that morning, I faked an upset stomach. The teacher sent me down to the nurse's office, located on the first floor just below my destination.

I hustled up the flight of stairs, taking two at a time. I hadn't eaten since the night before, and I was starving. All I could think of was getting my hands on that fat brown bag of goodies. As I reached the top of the stairs and rounded the corner, I spotted the gym teacher, Mr. Irwin, and the grade seven teacher, Mrs. Miller, standing outside her classroom chatting. My heart leapt into my throat. My first impulse was to turn and bust out of there, but I knew that any such move would only create suspicion, so I hurried past them while attempting to keep my composure and look as inconspicuous as possible.

The walk down the hall seemed like an eternity, and I could feel their piercing eyes on my back. Finally, I arrived at the end of the hall and rounded the corner, out of their sight. "Maybe they're on to me," I thought. It gave me the shivers to think so, and something inside warned me: "Don't go for it! Go back to class." It was my instincts. In later years, I grew to respect them, but at that time I was too immature to heed their ominous message.

After about five minutes, I heard the sound of a door closing and footsteps fading in the distance. I waited till all was silent and then peeped around the corner. All was clear, so I rushed the short distance to the locker, jerked it open, and snatched a big brown bag off the top shelf. As I did so, I complimented myself. "Chow time," I laughed.

Then "Jones!" A voice boomed down the hallway. "Is that your locker?"

I froze in my tracks. The towering presence of Mr. Irwin approached fast, and then he stood glaring down at me.

"Is this your locker?" he demanded.

His voice sent chills through me. The man knew damn well that it wasn't my locker. He knew he'd caught me red-handed, and I knew how a frightened animal in a trap must feel.

"So you're the one who's been stealing the lunches!"

There was nothing I could say. The evidence was in my hand.

He grabbed me roughly by the back of my collar and half-walked and half-dragged me through the hallway and down the stairs to the principal's office.

For the next half hour, I shook my way through some intense interrogation by our principal, Mr. Gibson, plus Mr. Irwin and my homeroom teacher, Mrs. Morden. It's a terrifying experience to have three adults yelling at and threatening an eight-year-old kid. There was no sense trying to explain how my brother's death had led to my bed-wetting problem, which had led to my hunger problem, which had led to my stealing problem. They were already convinced that I was a dirty little thief!

It was decided that, because Mr. Irwin was the one who'd caught me, he'd be the one to execute the punishment. I'd heard that he strapped the hardest of all the teachers, and the thought of it terrified me so badly I thought I might crap my pants. I cried, I pleaded, I begged for mercy.

I can't recall how many times he strapped me on each hand, but I do recall how painful it was and how I squealed like a pig going to slaughter. The rumours about Mr. Irwin were true, the dude could lay a whipping on you. No doubt I deserved being punished, but he went overboard. The palms of my hands were swollen and sore for days.

After the punishment, the principal ordered me straight home with a note for Ma, and, since she was a strong Christian woman who had no tolerance for stealing, I knew I was in for another good, old-fashioned whipping at home.

Instead of going straight home, I headed downtown to the penny arcade, where I stalled till after dark. I finally arrived home around seven o'clock. As soon as I walked through the front door, Barbara, sitting on the couch watching TV, looked up and whispered, "Charles, they know you stole all those lunches. Mr. Gibson phoned Ma."

"Get in here, boy!" Dad's stern voice boomed from the kitchen.

A bolt of fright shot through me, and I was a trembling mental wreck. I'd besmirched their good name, and I knew I was heading to my doom. Stealing was taboo, and none of my brothers or sisters had ever been in trouble before. I stopped just out of Dad's reach at the edge of the table. Ma and Dad glared at me in disgusted silence. I got the feeling that they were filled with revulsion by my very presence, and it made me feel cheap and worthless. Instead of a beating, they did a lot of yelling. Called me a dirty, rotten, no-good thief. The words hurt more than physical punishment would have. No normal kid intentionally tries to make his parents have a low opinion of him. I couldn't do anything but stand there, head bowed, weeping in shame.

My lunch bag-thieving career ended that day. However, I learned that when people perceive you as a thief it's a stigma that follows you around like a bad smell. Whenever something went missing at school after that, I became the prime suspect.

But thieving had gotten into my system! I found that I couldn't give it up. It was solving problems for me — hunger problems now and soon money problems as well.

A few mornings later, while on my way to school, I noticed a lady putting an empty milk bottle on the porch. In those days, most people had their milk, butter, and bread delivered to their homes. I thought, "That bottle is worth a nickel refund at the variety store next to school." Which meant a couple of bags of chips. I wrestled with my conscience for a few seconds, even felt some guilt, but wrong came out on top of right.

I doubled around the block, went down the alley, hopped the fence into the lady's backyard, and cased the area. Nobody was looking, so I slipped along the driveway and onto the front porch, grabbed the bottle, and ran like hell.

At the time, I had no idea that people left money — a quarter or fifty cents — in the bottle, the mailbox, or the milk box. My intention was simply to cash in the bottle at the variety store. It was while fleeing the scene that I heard the jingling of coins in the bottle. To my delight, I found fifty cents.

Over the next few years, I regularly scouted the neighbourhoods around the school. I had become exactly what my parents had called me: a sneaky little thief. But all guilt aside, it sure beat being hungry.

I got caught again for other "crimes," but after the first few school strap sessions I grew accustomed to the pain. I also discovered a way to give the teachers back a little pain. Our science teacher, Mr. Hill, was the meanest teacher in the school. He used to keep a little green file box with records of all his students. Each time you messed up in his class, it was documented in the green box. Mess up three times, and out came the strap. Mr. Hill thought I had a bad attitude, and he'd warned me on a few occasions that he was going to fix it with some of his special medicine. The worst thing about Mr. Hill was that he'd strap you in front of the class. He wasn't big and powerful like Mr. Irwin, but he could lay some hot sting on your hands.

One morning I was late. When I attempted to explain myself, he wouldn't hear of it. Ordered me to shut up, but I was too upset to control my emotions, and I continued to talk back. Next thing I knew he jerked me out of my seat and pulled me to the front of the class. He raised that old black strap way up over his head and brought it down full force. My timing had become impeccable through many strap sessions by then, and just as the strap was about to connect I pulled my hand back, and the strap went whizzing by and caught Mr. Hill flat on his upper thigh. It sounded like a firecracker going off. His face turned vivid red from the shot of pain, and he got to dancing around like he was on fire, which provoked the class into a burst of laughter. Old man Hill went ballistic then and gave it to me pretty good. Some landed, others missed. When it was over, we both had some pretty good welts on us.

According to my grade four report card, by then I had developed "behavioural problems," I was "aggressive," and I had an "attitude problem." After several more confrontations with classmates and trips down to the principal's office, it was decided that I should be put through a battery of psychological tests. After my promising start in kindergarten, my problems sidetracked me badly, and the conclusion was that I then had a "learning disability." Why it took them so long to discover it is beyond me, especially since Barb had stopped tutoring me long before, and I'd begun to have serious problems with reading and math back in grade two. Yet somehow I'd managed to reach grade four. Most of the time I slept or daydreamed my way through classes.

But they were right about my change in attitude. I was no longer the well-behaved and passive little boy I'd been just a few years earlier. I'd grown tired of being messed with, taunted, and bullied, and I was starting to get back in the faces of my antagonists. Except when it came to Red Turner. He still had my number.

Grade four was also about the time that I began to experience fits of rage. I'd become so angry that sometimes I'd inflict damage on myself. It usually occurred after a whipping or a reprimand. In our home, when you were told to shut up, either you did or you suffered the consequences. Often my emotions got the best of me. I'd get so fired up that it was difficult to slack off, so I was always getting cuffed by Ma. Also, I had a tendency to be hard on myself for messing up. I didn't know how to deal with my shortcomings. I'd storm out of the house to some secluded place and violently pound my face and call myself all kinds of degrading names. It was as though there was some hideous beast inside me fighting to escape. On some occasions, I beat my face so violently that it would bruise and swell. Then, when my rage eased, I'd seek out a place to whimper and pray to God for peace of mind. Those were frightening experiences.

The fact was I couldn't keep my mind on schoolwork — or *off* stealing — because I was preoccupied with the simple survival of my spirit.

CHAPTER 8

My Singing Debut

Even as things were going badly at school, Dad was still trying to reach me at home. When I was nine, he decided that I should get up and join him in the singing part of his church service.

One day my father and mother were singing in the house, and I just jumped in and got to singing with them, bellowing it out like I'd never done before. They were surprised at how my voice had developed. I'd been singing around the house for years. As far back as kindergarten, I used to sing "Jesus Loves Me," and the teachers would always comment, "My, Charles, what a beautiful voice you have!" That always made me feel good.

But that first time I got up to sing with Ma and Dad I was so nervous that I was shaking. 'Course now you can't get me to sit down and keep quiet, but that first time I had stage fright pretty bad. I was shakin' like a freshly caught sunfish when my dad said, "Brothers and sisters, we have a surprise this afternoon. We are blessed to have the young Charles Jones to bring us a blessing in song. Come on up here, son."

When he said that, I froze, but pleasing my father meant a lot to me, so I went through with it. Also, he'd always sneak a quarter on me when he wanted my cooperation, so you could say I made my professional singing debut that day at nine years old.

I stood up, and the elderly lady at the piano said, "Son, what key you going to sing in?"

I remember looking at her blankly. Key? How did I know what key I was going to sing in?

She said, "Just hum a bit for me, Charles."

I hummed a bit of "Just a Closer Walk with Thee," and she figured out what key I was in. She was a kind, churchgoing lady in a worn-out navy suit, one of those truly thankful Christians who didn't have much but was thankful for what little she had.

But once I got into it, the spirit took over, and I really cranked it. I remember shaking my head back and forth and looking skyward like Ma. I could hear voices of encouragement from the congregation: "Praise God!" and "Amen, brother" and "Hallelujah!" and "Sing it, Brother Jones."

After it was done, I felt terrific, like I was Frankie Lyman or Elvis Presley. I was hooked for good on performing. My dad was so full of pride that day, like he was whenever I got involved in things with him, like whenever I asked him questions about the Bible.

We began to spend more time than ever in the Lord's house. But for me, church was becoming more of a chore to attend than when I was younger. At four and five years old, I loved Sundays at church with the family, but by the time I was ten I was no longer a morning person. Suddenly, Sunday mornings were hell for the lazy kid I was becoming, and there were a dozen other places I'd rather have been than in some hot, stuffy church. My insomnia made it difficult to stay awake in church, and whenever Ma caught me drifting off a pinch on the leg brought me back to reality. A few minutes later, I was dozing off again.

I wasn't the only one tired either. Half the males in the congregation would be sawing logs, their heads lolled back, their mouths wide open, flies sitting on their thick lips. Then all of a sudden a loud snore, or a rip-roaring fart, would fill the air, followed by snickering. These were good Christian folk, but sometimes it's tough to keep your composure. Not that all found these eruptions amusing. There were the straitlaced, self-righteous among the congregation who viewed snoring and farting as mortal sins. Not that I agreed with cutting the cheese in the Lord's house, 'cause it sure did stink the place up. Especially in the hot summer when there was no breeze. The foul smell would linger in that old one-room church for ages.

A veteran of such church activities, Dad knew how to deal with most situations, and he could do it without missing a beat! If he saw someone nodding off, he'd continue as if he hadn't noticed a thing, and then suddenly, in the middle of a sentence, he'd pound the podium and holler in a thunderous voice some quote from scripture. "The FEAR of God is the BEGINNING of wisdom!" Man, those sleeping brothers would jump up as if somebody had stuck pins in their asses. It was hilarious, and most of the congregation really got a chuckle from it.

About that time, I also began to attend services with my

cousins at some of the big churches in Detroit, in particular at Reverend C.L. Franklin's New Bethel Baptist Church. The contrast was huge. My father's sermons were to a small bunch of God-fearing country folk; they dressed plainly and acted humbly and respectfully. They weren't into all the big city slicker hype, the bright lights, the showmanship. They went to church with one thing in mind, to give thanks for what they had. But when we went to C.L.'s church, it was a different scene. In those days, Aretha, C.L.'s daughter, wasn't yet a singing star, at least not a big-name entertainer, but she sure was a singing star in her dad's church. C.L. was one of the most flamboyant, charismatic ministers I've ever seen and one of the most powerful speakers I've ever heard. He was also a great friend of Martin Luther King.

We went to C.L.'s many times, and my dad spoke there on occasion as a guest pastor. When you went to Reverend Franklin's, it was more like going to the Twenty Grand show bar than to a church. It was a huge building with seating for maybe five hundred in the pews, plus hundreds more in the balconies. And it was filled every Sunday. The scale of the place and the massive stained-glass windows always impressed me. And C.L. didn't have just a few singers and an old piano like Dad had at North Buxton. No, C.L. brought in big bands, whole orchestras even, with special guest performers backed by a thunderous B-3 organ and guitars and trumpets. He put on quite a show!

Later C.L. built an even bigger church on Detroit's west side near Hastings. He then brought in even bigger gospel acts — all the biggest gospel names in America: Lou Rawls with the Soulstirrers, whose lead singer was a handsome young guy named Sam Cooke; the Five Blind Boys; the

Staple Singers; Della Reese; and, more frequently, of course, Aretha. Even then you could see that this girl could sing and had star quality.

Younger people especially went to Reverend Franklin's services because they were "in," trendy. You might have been at the Twenty Grand or the Fox Theater on Saturday night partying, but come Sunday morning you had to get out to Franklin's gig. Unfortunately, showboat congregations like C.L.'s got caught up more in the hype of the messenger and, in my opinion, lost the essential message. Entertainment became the major part of the worship service.

There were also preachers in Detroit living large off their congregations. They cruised around town in luxury cars, lived in expensive homes, and wore the sharpest threads the congregations' money could buy. Meanwhile, many of the churchgoers were off the 'hood and were so poor that the rats in their houses were on welfare. Yet, come Sunday, these poor folks were in church handing their hard-earned cash over to some pimpy preacher prostituting the word of God.

I knew such a minister in Detroit. The man was such a crook he should have worn a ski mask. When it came to taking in money, I never saw anybody who could work a flock the way he did. He'd make his grand entrance onto the stage from his study, wearing a long, flowing black silk robe. The choir would just be finishing a rousing gospel number, and here he'd come strutting across the stage in his gown like he was the Anointed One. The robe was a brilliant move; it gave him a divine appearance.

"Brothers and sisters in Christ," he'd say, looking out over his assemblage with the most sanctified look he could muster. "It's time to give some blessings back to our sweet

Jesus!" He'd be bold about it too. He'd holler and pound the podium. "I don't want to hear nothing but silence hit the offering plate! No jingle! Just the quiet stuff!" He'd gaze down on his congregation like he was the good Lord himself. "Can you hear the Lord speaking to your heart tonight?" he'd whisper into the microphone. Then he'd stop. The place would get so quiet you could have heard a dime drop, except no one dared to drop a mere dime.

Then he'd start singling people out, get the guilt trip going good. "I know the Lord's laid a blessing on the Baker and Brown families this past week!" He'd pause for a few seconds, look around the church, then carry on. "Brother Brown and Brother Baker, you been working overtime at the Ford plant, and you gonna get the bills paid this month! Good God Almighty," he'd yell and dance across the stage. "The Browns and the Bakers gonna pay bills and feed the family this week! Ain't God good?" Soon the entire church would be jumping up and down and rejoicing. Then, suddenly, he'd stop dancing and cast an admonishing look out over his flock. "But if Brother Brown and Brother Baker hold back on their tithing, they're cheating the Lord!"

That's a heavy trip to lay on any God-fearing person. Fills you with guilt and fear. The Browns, the Bakers, and everybody else in that church would be squirming in their seats and coughing up their cash.

I'm thankful Dad wasn't one of those greedy preachers. All he ever wanted to do was spread the good word. He always said he'd get his reward in the sweet by-and-by.

About that time, I also began working weekends in Uncle Roy's barbershop off 12th Street, in Blackbottom — what

everyone called Detroit's downtown black area. If you're
into gossiping or debating, then black barbershops are the
place to be. I'd be sweeping hair off the floor and shining
shoes, pretending to be hard at work, but all the while I'd be
checking out the conversations. If you weren't hip to these
guys, you'd swear by the adversarial way they went at each
other that they were sworn enemies.

There'd be all kinds of disputes going on simultaneously.
"Who da best ballplayer you ever saw?" somebody would
yell. My dad loved baseball with a passion, even played some
semipro around the border cities. He'd holler, "Willie
Mays!" And they'd all be hollering loud and drawing a
crowd, laughing and arguing up a storm. The key was that
whoever shouted the loudest assumed his opinion had won
out. My uncle would really ride them. "Ah, y'all niggahs
must be out of y'all minds!" Then the place would explode
in laughter.

My favourite debates were the ones about boxing. In
those days in Detroit, there were fight cards at least once a
month at the Olympia or at Cobo Hall. When the topic
turned to boxing, you knew it was going to get bombastic.

"Joe Louis would have kicked Sonny Liston's backside,"
my dad would say, just to get things going.

"Are you crazy, Matches!" Uncle Roy would shoot back.
Matches was his nickname for Dad because of his fiery temper as a kid. "Liston was too big, too strong, for Joe. He'd 've
run Joe's black ass right outta da ring!"

I loved it when they got into the best pound-for-pound
debate. Arguments could last for hours, even days.

Most of the time, the debates were just good "jive-time"
barbershop hot air. However, when the topic got around to

politics, there was a drastic change. That's when hostility would rear its ugly head. It was clear to me even as a teenager that these men harboured a deep resentment toward the white establishment. Later, as I grew older, I came to understand why. Deprivation is the big daddy of discontentment, and with it come resentment and hostility. It's a natural reaction from folks who've grown weary of living in rat- and roach-infested homes and welfare projects. As a black ghetto kid, as I grew older, I began to notice the world outside my existence. I saw others grabbing up nice slices of the pie, while we were left scuffling among one another for a few of the crumbs.

Exclusion tends to leave you bitter, and my bitterness was starting to awaken.

CHAPTER 9

Hitting Back!

One day the unexpected happened at school, and the darkness that was overtaking me brightened for a while.

Sometimes in class there weren't enough textbooks to go around, so during certain periods students were paired off to share them. When reading period was announced, the stampede was on! It looked more like a sports event than reading time with thirty kids shoving and fighting to share desks with their friends. But nobody came near me, which didn't bother me (I knew I stank up a breeze), but the fact was I actually looked forward to reading classes. Not that I liked reading so much, but it was my time to daydream. I'd be riding the trail with the Lone Ranger, making a sensational Willie Mays catch, or maybe knocking out the heavyweight champion of the world. I was allowed to escape for a while.

It was during one of these breaks from reality that there was a knock on the door. The principal entered, followed by a slender, beautiful girl with long, flowing blonde hair and a gorgeous smile. He introduced her as Karen and explained that she'd just moved up from Miami Beach. I was knocked over like a ten-pin bowling pin. Man, was she gorgeous!

The teacher suggested that Karen select someone to share a desk with. As it was, I was the only one in the class who hadn't paired off. She glanced around the room, and eventually her eyes rested on me. Thank God I was sitting down, or else I'd have fainted. Next thing I knew she slid in beside me, which made me feel extremely uncomfortable because of my offensive odour. My first urge was to get up and run. "Somebody must have put her up to this cruel joke," I thought. "Why else would this angelic-looking creature descend to my level?"

She turned to me, smiled, and whispered "Hi." She sounded sincere, and I sensed a nice vibe from her. I don't know who was rattled more by my unbelievable luck — me or my classmates. If looks could have killed, I definitely would have been among the recently departed. But I didn't care what they thought anymore. Besides, I was fascinated by the smooth skin, the long blonde hair, and the sweet scent of this divine apparition seated beside me. I was completely under her spell.

She even spoke to me. I learned that her father was a construction engineer who built bridges and that her family had moved around a lot. She'd attended schools in Portland, Baltimore, Chicago, Montreal, and Miami. During her travels, she'd been exposed to various cultures, including blacks, which explained why she didn't have a problem with me.

Over the next few months, I discovered we both shared a passion for music. We also enjoyed dancing, and we even entered a couple of dance contests. It was just be-bopping around, never any of that cheek-to-cheek stuff. We were just good friends. But it didn't matter that our relationship was strictly platonic — it still stirred up plenty of jealousy, especially among Red and his boys. None of them could dance to save his ass, so they stood around like a group of loud-mouthed delinquents trying to outdo each other by making crude remarks.

By late spring of 1957, Cupid's arrow had struck home, and I'd become an obsequious lackey for Karen. She consumed my thoughts. I imagined we were going steady. I fantasized that we were dancing slowly to romantic tunes, that she thought I was the coolest dude on the planet. In the reality department, just carrying her books was the highlight of my day.

Our relationship brought some positive changes. I began to take pride in my appearance. Every morning I'd be sure to wash, comb my hair, and even wear clean underwear — when they were available.

Karen's appeal went far beyond physical appearance. Karen possessed a rare sweetness that drew people to her. Red Turner included. He began to put on a phoney front around her and acted as if he and I were cool. In fact, he treated me so kindly that she found it difficult to believe he was a jerk. I attempted to get her hip to Red's real ways, but she brushed it off as if I was exaggerating. Red was one slick, conniving dude. I figured that sooner or later Karen would get a real peep at his whole card and find out the truth about him. Wishful thinking!

Fate can be capricious and brutal. Here I was willing to move heaven and Earth for Karen . . . and she got all hung up on Red. Man, I was devastated when she told me that she really dug Red and that they were going on a date.

Once Red got the upper hand, he went back to his taunting and bullying ways.

Then I flunked grade four, Karen and Red moved on to grade five, and I returned to my old defeated ways. I slipped back into daydreaming to close out the world. The days of hanging out with Karen during recess and at lunchtime were gone. No more kicking it together at the dances either. Red had those bases all covered now.

On the streets, when a brother gets hung up on a lady, they say, "She's got your nose open." If that's the case, then Karen had mine so wide open a Mack truck could have pulled up and found a place to park. The more I saw them together, the more my animosity grew toward Red. My emotions, my thoughts, my anger, were taking me to a place I'd never been before. Revenge was filling my thoughts.

That summer my father had grown tired of me coming home beaten and bloody, so he hustled me to the Police Athletic Boxing League, where a friend of his named Mickey Warner trained boxers. At ten, I was the youngest kid in the gym, and the first day Warner tossed me into the ring with a twelve year old. My only consolation was that, like me, the other kid had never boxed before. Mickey put old, sweaty headgear on me, tied on some big, sixteen-ounce gloves, shoved in a mouthpiece, then pushed me toward the centre of the ring. I was nervous, but the other kid came out swinging like a windmill, and instinct took over. I began swinging back for the first time, and it gave me an exhilarating feeling. We boxed three one-minute rounds and didn't get hurt, but this introduction to the sweet science had a profound effect on me. I *liked* being able to defend myself! I *liked* hitting back when I was attacked!

I worked out determinedly over the summer of 1957, and I discovered that boxing was something I was actually good at. I also shot up a couple of inches in height and gained a few pounds. The boxing lessons, plus a lot of sparring and a bit of a gain in size, elevated my confidence to a level that I'd never known before.

Dad also had a friend named Duke Ellis who trained fighters out of the Big D, Detroit's most famous boxing gym, and I also began to hang out there. Joe Louis used to come to Detroit and drop by the gym sometimes. Joe usually came in for one of the fight cards at the Olympia, where he might be asked to do some colour commentary or appear in one fighter's corner for a few bucks. While in town, he used to like to visit some of the older trainers he knew, like Teddy McWhorters, who went on to become Canadian Heavyweight Champion George Chuvalo's trainer. Through Teddy, I got to meet Joe, and a couple of times promoter Andy Brown let me tag along as he drove Joe to personal appearances. When Dad heard that I was riding and hanging with Joe Louis, my sorry stock with him took a turn upward.

I was also beginning to feel as if I was one bad dude. I even got into a couple of fights in the park that summer — and won! The gym became like a second home and gave me a sense of belonging for the first time, and, oddly, the thing I enjoyed almost as much as the boxing itself was the luxury of being able to take a shower. It was the first time I felt like I was privileged, like I was a member of a classy club.

By the fall of 1957, I was almost as big as Red Turner was, and I could rumble with any of his boys. Now most of them cut me slack unless he was around to defend them. Nevertheless, I was still scared of Red, and when he taunted me I still let it slide. But inside, my hatred for him was eating away at me. I wanted to fight him badly. I almost did a few times, but fear kept holding me back, and I ended up steering clear of him and his turf.

But even on my own turf, I couldn't avoid attacks. Windsor's blacks were victims of the bigoted times, which left a lot of kids mean, angry, and hostile. On too many occasions, we took it out on one another. You couldn't pass through the park or along street corners without somebody trying to punk you out. The bars that blacks frequented often resembled Dodge City, particularly on the weekends, and few weekends passed when somebody wasn't stabbed or beaten.

There was little in the way of respect among us. The only thing that kept them off you was fear. The crazier you acted, the more they feared you, and the more room they gave you. Eventually, crazy became my featured act.

When you hung on the street corners, or even passed by certain dudes, you had to be ready for trouble. Groups of guys would be standing around shucking, jiving, and shouting all kinds of offensive names and insults at one another. If you weren't strong enough to stand up, you either got fronted out or got your ass kicked.

The first time I got it on with another black kid was with an older kid named Harry who lived a couple of blocks away. Ma had sent me to the corner store for milk, but going near the place always made me nervous because tough kids hung out front, and they were always bullying us younger dudes.

As I was passing, Harry sounded on me. "Hey, Jones! Your hair's nappy just like your pappy!"

I knew Harry was a bully, but I'd never had trouble with him before, so I figured we were cool. I fired back, "Hey, brother! Just because your breath stinks like ape shit don't mean you're Tarzan!"

"I can tell by your hair, your daddy's a bear!" he hollered back.

He was playing a game blacks call getting into the dozens. It's where we sound off on each other's relatives, especially on the other person's parents. You keep firing off one insult after another until one of you gives in to anger. The other dudes got off on the exchange, and they were slapping each other some skin.

I didn't dig anybody putting my daddy down, so I jumped on his mother's case. "Man, your mama's so fat she's got to go to the junkyard just to get her ass weighed!"

All the guys busted up laughing, and I felt cool. I had fronted him big time.

Before he could respond, I reeled off another one. "Hey, man," I yelled. "Your breath stinks so bad your teeth done packed up and left you."

It was a bad move. Harry had the worst-looking, greenest teeth you'd ever want to see. Looked like ragweed, and he was supersensitive about them. Next thing I knew, we were into it. I found myself boxing his ass off just like I'd been taught in the gym. I hit him some good, straight left jabs, and the cat just didn't know how to contend with me. Eventually, a couple of older guys stepped in and broke it up. Harry's nose was bleeding, and I was busting with a newfound pride. I'd just dusted a guy much bigger and older than me. Man, I was starting to happen!

But at school, things only got worse.

I flunked grade four again, but my new defiance and confidence had changed me. I became aggressive. For so long, I'd been passive and docile, but now I was becoming confrontational. I started to live up to my label as a "problem" student, but from my perspective I felt as if I was fighting for mere survival. One July day I was on the way home from the Peerless Dairy when four white kids attacked me over an ice-cream cone. One slashed me with a razor, which left a jagged, five-stitch scar on my wrist. I was getting *sick* of the harassment everywhere I turned.

Red Turner was still bigger than I was, and he still had me bluffed, calling me the usual names in front of his friends: nigger, spook, coon. One day he forced me to fight one of his friends for his own amusement. I tried to resist, but Turner made it clear that, if I didn't fight the other kid, I'd have to face Turner himself. He was still too strong for me to attempt that, so I reluctantly fought the other boy. When I began getting the best of the fight, Turner stepped in and gave me a beating anyway.

When I got home, I had to admit once again to my dad that, yes, I'd taken a beating and that, no, I hadn't been able to defend myself.

On my own turf, things were little better. One day a couple of bigger black kids walked past our house and began tossing insults about my mother. I'd taken a lot of abuse directed at me in the past, but when they started getting on about my mother I finally blew. This time I fought a wild but hopeless fight against the two of them. For my efforts, I got two broken ribs from being kicked while I was on the ground. It was my first experience with broken bones.

But I was getting bigger, and I wasn't buying the pacifist line any longer. My rage was continuing to build. Then it all came to a head one day. The anger that had been festering inside for years exploded against Red Turner.

CHAPTER 10

The Ding-Dong Class

One day I bumped into Karen on the way to school, and she invited me to walk with her. My first thought was of Red, but he was nowhere in sight, and she was looking fine, so we began walking and talking. The next thing I knew I was carrying her books, and her arm was hooked in mine. It was cool being with her again. After we reached school, she pecked me on the cheek, and we went our separate ways.

I never thought anymore about it, but some of Red's crew had seen us together, and after the news reached his ears the word went out that Red was looking to relieve me of my breathing rights! I was scared stiff the rest of the morning.

Later that day he caught up with me in class. "Hey, Jones, you stupid nigger!"

The words froze me.

"I told you to keep your black ass away from Karen, didn't I?"

I turned and looked into the hatred of Turner's cold

blue eyes. The chilling glare sent my heart racing, but this time I defiantly returned his stare. I was tired of being bullied and humiliated by this turkey. My fear was being overtaken by rage.

Red yanked me right out of my desk. "You black bastard! I warned you not to mess with my girl!" He shoved me bouncing off a couple of desks and onto the floor.

On the way down, the back of my head struck a desk, leaving me stunned for a moment, but before Red could come at me my head cleared, and I leapt off the floor, and, like a man possessed, I began lashing out at his face with both fists. He went down, bleeding and squealing for mercy, but I stayed on him and kept pounding. It began to feel like a weird dream; I remember hearing muffled voices in the background, too faint to distinguish. I was in a frenzy, and the only thing I could see and hear was the thumping sound of my fists making Turner's face all bloody. Suddenly, a powerful pair of hands pulled me back and flung me against the wall, and I was jarred back to reality by the face of Mr. Irwin.

"Don't move!" he commanded, pointing at me. "I'll take care of you in a minute."

This time his words brought no fear to me, although I did as he'd ordered and stood back and watched as he and another teacher tended to Red. Turner was hustled off to the nurse's office for repairs, while I was dragged down to the principal's office. There Mr. Irwin freaked out and called me a damned hoodlum, a troublemaker, a danger to society, and a number of other things. I didn't even attempt to explain my side of the story. He wasn't interested. His mind was set, he had written me off as bad, and I wrote him off as just another part of my problem.

I was "punished" with one of his dreaded strap sessions, but by then I was so full of rebellion that, no matter how many times he struck me, I refused to cry. Inside I felt a deep sense of pride for having stood up to a bully who'd tormented me for years and for taking the best whupping Mr. Irwin could dish out without giving him the satisfaction of seeing me cry. I made a promise to myself in that moment that nobody was *ever* going to pick on me again. If someone messed with me, I'd find *any* means to win.

The worst part of the whole affair wasn't the strap; it was Karen's reaction. Karen became aloof with me after that. A few months later, she moved to Vancouver, and I never saw her again.

A few days after the incident with Red, my further "punishment" was to be transferred to another school, one that dealt with "problem children" and "slow learners": Harry E. Guppy Public School. Even the name was a humiliation. I was put in a remedial class that everyone called the "ding-dong class." The teaching standards were certainly lower, but the ridicule and racial tauntings, if anything, ratcheted up. Most of my classmates came from a troubled past, and we were viewed as outcasts. We got razzed by the regular students, and the taunts provoked me into more fights, which led to more strap sessions.

The wounds I inflicted on Red were only superficial; he healed and carried on with his life. Mine, however, were deep emotional scars that haunted me for years because I'd been banished to the ding-dong class. Red had provoked me for years, yet I was the one who paid the price for finally standing up for myself.

Things continued downhill fast after that, and that's

when I began my gang career. I was never forced to join a gang; I just kind of gravitated toward it.

I'd reached a stage where I rebelled against and questioned *everything* — everything I was told at school, everything my parents said to me. It seemed as though we were in endless conflict at home. My mother would be hollering at me one minute and crying the next. Dad and I couldn't agree on anything anymore. He'd get mad at me and threaten to whip my ass, but he seldom followed through with it. I guess he either gave up on me or just figured it wouldn't do any good. He was right. By then, I had lost all fear of being whipped. If the punishment was sending me to my room, I'd just climb out the window and cut out for downtown. It used to get so intense around the house that most of the time I avoided going home until there was no place else to go. Most of all, I disliked abiding by their rules. By thirteen, the lure of the streets had grown so strong that I wanted complete freedom to do as I chose. I didn't give a damn about the grief or misery I was laying on my parents.

My older cousin Sonny was a gang member, and, man, I thought he was the coolest cat on Earth. His gang was called the Mercer Street Boys, from our street on which most of them lived, and I began tagging along with them. When I first started hanging around the corners, I stayed as inconspicuous as possible. These guys were tough, and a lot of them had bad attitudes, but they knew I was Sonny's blood, so they pretty much left me alone.

The leader was a dude named Ducky, who was Sonny's best friend. He was short and stocky, with broad shoulders and huge hands. He was super quick, with a mean streak and the heart of a warrior. And it didn't matter how big or bad you thought you were: mess with Ducky, and you'd better be able to get it on.

Most of the time, the Mercer Street Boys simply hung out on the corners guzzling cheap bootlegged dandelion wine. At seventy-five cents a bottle, getting drunk was easy. After a few swigs, our spirits would rise, and we'd get to jamming tunes. I was fascinated by the way they sang and danced. Some were really gifted singers, and I wanted to show them how I could chirp too.

One night, after I'd been around a couple of weeks, I got the chance. They were singing this tune called "In the Still of the Night." The lead was being performed by a dude name Greasy, a nickname he'd earned because he packed his hair down with black shoe polish to make it look slick and shiny, like Little Richard's. Sometimes Greasy got so carried away performing that he'd perspire, and the black shoe polish would melt and stream down his forehead. Man, then he *really* looked greasy! As they neared the end of the song, Greasy began to strain a bit; he couldn't quite reach the high notes. I was a little nervous, but I jumped in and hit them notes. Attention turned to me, and I was afraid they'd think I was playing them, but when Sonny slapped me some skin and said "Sing it, little cousin," I knew I was being accepted. After that, I was on the corner jamming whenever possible.

The first time I witnessed a gang fight was when Ducky took on a biker dude named Trash. Until then, I'd never seen anybody with enough courage to stand up to the motorcycle gang members who cruised Windsor in those days with swastikas on their vests. Whether or not they actually subscribed to Hitler's theories of Aryan superiority, I don't know, but they sure used the word *nigger* a lot.

On more than one occasion, while we were hanging downtown, they'd wheel past and holler out racial slurs. Not that the bikers had a monopoly on racial venom. As often as not, ordinary white kids cruising down the main drag would shout out racial slurs and insults as well. Back then, it was the fashionable thing to do. Wasn't nothing for us to yell back either. But when the bikers did it, I was too intimidated to respond. I knew damn well they were looking for any lame excuse to whip my ass. So I just kept on trucking as though I never heard them. Back then, I firmly believed that most whites hated blacks. Even the ones who smiled in my face I didn't trust. I know differently now, but when I was a kid precious few were showing me otherwise.

One Saturday night, the Mercer Street Boys had just left a dance and were heading to a restaurant called the Detroit Grill. Ducky and Sonny were holding hands with a couple of foxy white girls they'd met at the dance. We were singing tunes and just kicking around having a good time when the rumble of motorcycles began to drown out our voices. As the bikes came nearer, the noise became so loud we could barely hear ourselves. I felt shivers. My instincts warned me of trouble. A group of maybe a dozen bikers were converging on us.

As they came alongside, they slowed to a crawl. They stared and gunned their motors — a bravado manoeuvre intended to intimidate us. For me, their effort was a waste of time because I was already shaking like a leaf in a storm. Not so for Ducky and the boys. They glared back, and so, as scared as I was, I stared back too. Not that I had any intention of provoking them. I was just following along.

Over the years, I'd heard how bad these dudes could be.
How crazy and tough they were. I was fascinated by the sight
of them, but I was most intrigued by the brawny dude at the
front of the pack. He was dressed in a black T-shirt stretched
tightly across a thick chest, tight-fitting jeans, and a scruffy
black leather vest, and he had these massive arms covered
with tattoos. I figured he must be one superbad cat to be
leading this band of wild hombres. He eased his chopper to
the curb.

Sonny whispered to Ducky, "That's Trash Blake!"

My heart just about jumped into my mouth. Trash had a
reputation for being one of the most dangerous dudes in the
border cities. A few weeks earlier, he'd reportedly knocked
out two big black American dudes at a dancehall with one
punch each. My first reaction was to run. I figured the rest
of the guys were going to light out any second, and being the
slowest I needed a good headstart.

"Man, I know who it is!" Ducky sneered, looking indig-
nant.

His remark caught me off guard. If he knew who Trash
was, then why was he messing with him? I figured he must
have had a death wish to challenge this crazy dude.

"Hey, Trash," Ducky called out, inching closer to the
curb. "What yah lookin' at, you fool? You got a problem?"

"Yeah, nigger, I got a problem," Trash growled. "I don't
dig nigger-loving sluts." He pointed his finger in the direction of the girls and simulated a handgun and said, "Nigger,
nigger, pull the trigger. Bang! Bang!" That drew loud cheers
and laughter from his friends.

Ducky freaked out. "You chickenshit honky! Bring your
ass over here and say that."

Trash's face twitched, and his eyes began to bug out. He wasn't used to people standing up to him like that. "Time to do some coon hunting," he snarled.

"Don't sing it! Bring it, sucker!" Ducky challenged.

Trash fixed his stare on Ducky, kicked his stand down, and dismounted his Harley. "Nigger," he snorted, "I'm going to tap-dance all over your black face!"

Sonny shoved me away and said, "Split, little cousin." Then he reached into his pocket and flashed a blade and yelled, "This is between Ducky and Trash. Anybody jumps in, and I'll cut them a new asshole!"

But I was too fascinated to split. I stayed beside Sonny.

"Let's see what you got, coon," Trash smirked, motioning Ducky to bring it.

Ducky moved quickly off the curb to meet him, and the difference in size was huge. I figured Ducky was toast. Trash stood about six foot two and weighed well over two hundred, while Ducky was five foot ten and weighed in around 175. Trash roared into Ducky swinging with both hands and looking to smoke him fast. Dancing from side to side, Ducky dodged the blows and shot out two quick left jabs that landed solidly on Trash's chin. Then he moved out of range as Trash fired back wildly.

"That all you got, paddy boy?" Ducky taunted. "You too damn slow."

Rage distorted Trash's face.

I reached over and jerked on Sonny's arm. "Man, you got to do something before this cat kills Ducky."

But Sonny seemed to be strangely unrattled. Without taking his eyes off the fight, he placed a hand on my shoulder. "Relax, babe. It ain't happening. Ducky's gonna dust this honky's ass good."

Trash charged at Ducky like an enraged bull, throwing wild punches from all angles, any one of them with enough dynamite to knock Ducky sillier than The Three Stooges. But Ducky was fast on his feet, and he slipped away from the blows again with surprising ease. As I watched, fear began to disappear, and I began to appreciate Ducky's fighting techniques, how easily Ducky handled a much larger opponent. He was lightning fast, and his speed was confusing Trash. I listened to how he taunted and degraded big Trash and how much that got him off his game. I began to understand the psychological aspect of fighting. It takes more than big muscles to win.

Suddenly, Ducky lashed out with a rapid combination of left jabs and short right hands, most landing flush on Trash's beak, and Trash tumbled backward and then fell to one knee, blood gushing from both his nostrils. Ducky rushed forward and gave him a violent kick to the head that made a loud splat and sent blood spraying in an arc as Trash's head recoiled. Trash slumped to the pavement on his back. It made me sick to see it, but at the same time I was relieved it wasn't Ducky on the wrong end of a boot.

The other bikers were so stunned that they stood there in silence. Ducky jumped back, threw his hands in the air, and issued a challenge to them all, but nobody wanted any part of him. They scurried to pull Trash out of range and then did a full retreat.

I learned a valuable lesson that night: just because a dude has big arms doesn't mean he's tough. It's not how big you are but the size of your heart that counts. I'd later battle both in the ring and in the street with many guys who were bigger than I was, and a lot of them pumped iron to look big and intimidating, but they couldn't get their hearts to grow, so there wasn't much fight in them.

In later years, I learned to use this knowledge by fighting to overcome challenges that looked big and tough but really weren't.

CHAPTER 11

Big Jim

About the same time I began to hang with my gang buddies, I also launched my thieving career in a big way.

These days you hear a lot about on-line shopping. That's old news! I was on-line shopping back when the word *coke* meant a drink and a *joint* was a place where we hung out. In the 1960s, electric appliances were luxuries most ordinary homes didn't have. Not having clothes dryers, folks would hang their laundry on clotheslines overnight to dry, which is how my version of on-line shopping got going. I'd wait till my parents turned in and then slip out of my bedroom window and into nearby neighbourhoods to raid the lines for whatever clothes I needed: blue jeans, T-shirts, shirts, sweatshirts, you name it. I was on-line shopping before the Internet was even thought of.

Most nights I'd head for the corner to hang with the crew. One night they asked me if I wanted to make a few bucks. Next thing I knew I was standing at the edge of some alley in downtown Windsor keeping an eye out for the police. Suddenly, I heard the sound of breaking glass, and a few seconds later they all raced by me hollering, "Run, nigger, run!" We rushed across the street and into another long, dark alley before I fully realized what had gone down. They'd smashed the windows of a store and snatched some radios and small appliances.

The next night Ducky laid five bucks on me, my end of the previous night's take. It blew my mind! Five dollars! That was big dough for a thirteen year old. The last time I had that kind of cash in my pocket I had to work part time for a week cleaning ashes out of stokers. After that heist, I took part in many smash-and-grab jobs, sometimes hitting jewellery stores and snatching up real valuables such as rings, watches, chains, and necklaces.

I began to tag along and "keep six" during most of these jobs. Keeping six meant being the lookout guy. At first, I wasn't allowed to go with them during the dump to the fence, but after a while they grew to trust me, and one night I was introduced to a man called Big Jim, Windsor's biggest receiver of stolen goods.

As soon as we got our hands on hot goods, we went looking for Jim. Often we saw him parked somewhere, lying back, his arm hanging out the window, just waiting for business to come along. We'd approach and say, "Big Jim, can we talk to you for a minute?"

And Jim would say in his soft, croaky voice, "Whaddya got, kid?" His favourite line.

"Jim, we got these two radios here."

"Lemme have a look." And he'd snatch the goods and rotate them appraisingly as if they were lost gems.

I also remember many a time going to Jim's back door, two blocks from our house. Always to the back door. I'd knock, and Jim would shuffle to the torn, old, rusted-out screen in a sleeveless T-shirt, with a beer in one hand and a toothpick rolling around his lips.

"Jim, I got some stuff here."

"Whaddya got, kid?"

Sometimes, in the middle of the night, you couldn't even see Jim. He'd be just a disembodied voice from the darkness inside, and he'd shoo us away. "Not tonight, kid, they're watching." On those nights, Jim would sit in his dark house and just watch the street because the cops had his place under surveillance.

But most nights there'd be a constant knocking on Big Jim's side door, and his place would be lit up like main street. Nobody was allowed to answer the door but him. If I happened to be at Jim's, sitting inside, I would sometimes hear Jim talking in hushed tones at the side door, and then he and others would disappear into the basement. After business was conducted, the new arrivals would head upstairs to Jim's main floor, where they'd blow their money on booze and card games, which always seemed to be going on.

One afternoon I was hanging around the pool hall when Jim dropped in and asked me to go for a spin. Next thing I knew we were cruising around Riverside, an affluent section of town, and Jim was pointing at all these big homes and speculating about all the nice things inside them. He lectured me on how rich folks and their kids didn't give a damn about poor kids like me. He was very subtle and not overtly suggesting anything. But he was instilling ideas.

The next Friday evening, about six of us cruised the same area. In those days, most families did their shopping on Friday evenings, so if we spotted a house with no car in the driveway and no lights on inside it was a prospective hit. We'd cruise around the block a couple of times and case it out. If we thought it was a hot prospect, we'd pull up the street and park. That's when I'd go into action. I'd go up to the house and knock hard on the front door. If I heard stirring inside, I'd light out of there like hell. But if the house was clear, I'd signal the guys, and we'd bust in, usually by breaking a basement window, and I'd crawl in and open the back door.

The first time I was involved in a B and E I was thirteen. The house was huge, about ten times the size of the crib we lived in. It was the closest thing to a mansion I'd ever seen. At first, I was scared to death, but after a few minutes my nerves began to settle. It was my first glimpse at how the wealthy lived, and it blew my mind. We ransacked every room, taking booze, clothes, radios, TVs, and cash. On the way out, we raided the freezer and found a bunch of steaks. Later that evening, after we unloaded our goods at Big Jim's, we breezed over to a house we called The Ranch because it was where the Mercer Street Boys hung out, and the lady who lived there, Marie, cooked up the steaks. It was my first steak, and, Lordy, did I ever get hooked! After that, whenever we hit a house, I made certain to swing with some prime beef.

I knew that what I was doing was wrong, but guilty thoughts never entered my mind. All I knew was I had discovered a quick and easy way to make some cash. Plus there was something exciting about invading homes and taking possessions you'd only dreamed of having. I felt like James

Bond or Shaft on a mission. These raids also gave me a brief insight into how the other side lived.

Feuds were a constant feature of gang life, and one of the Mercer Street Boys' most violent feuds was with a gang called the Motor City Shakers, one of the most feared gangs in Detroit. On weekends, they'd cross into Windsor and show up at dances and house parties to romance our women; anyone who didn't like it got whipped upon. Ever since I could remember, they had the Windsor boys running scared. That all changed one night following the brutal beating of a younger brother of one of our members.

At the Windsor Arena one Sunday evening during roller skating, three Shakers confronted a kid named Kenny in the washroom and did a number on him, stomping and pounding him. It was about fifteen minutes before closing, and we wanted to beat it to the Detroit Grill to get a booth before it got too jammed. Ducky, Sonny, and I were just about to head out the back entrance when we spotted Kenny stumbling down the hall covered in blood.

Ducky took a look at Kenny's facial wounds. "What the hell happened?"

Kenny was in tears as he told us how three Shakers had jumped him over talking to a girl. The thought of these dudes just waltzing into our turf and doing whatever they chose really pissed us off.

"Let's find them dirty bastards," Ducky said.

We worked our way through the crowd, rounding up members of our gang and anybody else who wanted in. In all, we ended up with about twenty, most of whom were Mercer Street Boys. Then a girl came rushing up to tell us that a group of Shakers were in the front lobby. We hurried toward the front, and as we rounded the corner we spotted close to a dozen of them near the exit. They were wearing bandannas, the trademark of the gang.

Ducky strolled up cool as a cucumber and suckered one of them with a vicious right to the face. Poor soul was out before he hit the floor. Then both sides began swinging and kicking at each other. There wasn't much I could do but stand by and watch the action. I was both fascinated and terrified. It was pretty much unknown territory to me. I'd seen some fights but nothing like this. The Shakers were badly outnumbered and were on the wrong end of what was a very vicious brawl. They'd always been tough in numbers, or with weapons in their hands, but I wasn't surprised that in the bare-knuckle department our guys were superior.

There was no way the Shakers were going to win this battle, so one of them pulled a blade. Until that moment, I'd just been standing there and taking in the battle, but when the guy with the knife went after one of our guys, Vampire, whose back was turned, there was no time to think.

I rushed at the dude swinging my roller skates. One skate caught him on the arm and sent the knife flying. I swung the skates again, and they bounced off his shoulder. But my efforts weren't doing a lot to discourage him. He got his hand back on the knife and came up like he was going to slice me. The look in his eyes was pure evil. I was his meat! But by this time, the adrenaline had kicked in, and I moved into what is called the fighting zone, a state where you block out fear and pain.

"Come to Daddy," he growled. "I'm gonna cut your ass too thin to fry and just right to die!"

I'll never forget those words or the look in his eyes. He
meant business.

I charged at him and swung the skates again with all my might. The blow landed on his wrist, forcing him to drop the knife again. Then, on my next swing, I caught him squarely on the chin with the wheels, which sliced open a deep wound. He stumbled back a few steps and dropped to his knees. I had every intention of busting his head wide open, but, as I was about to bring the skates down again, he looked up at me. His eyes were glassy, and blood was gushing from the wound. He was in no position to defend himself, and something stopped me from going any further.

"Get the hell outta here before I kill you!" I yelled, trying to sound as crazed as I could.

He rose slowly and backed up, all the while keeping his eyes on me, then turned and fled through the front exit. He seemed to be surprised that I'd let him slide. Where he came from, mercy was scarcer than an honest politician, but for me there was nothing noble in pounding a person when he's finished.

Before it was all over, we chased the Shakers right down to the Detroit River, and some of them actually dove into the water to escape us.

After that brawl, I became hooked on street fighting. Winning fights elevated my self-esteem. And each new win filled me with more confidence. With it also came the slaps on the back and the words of praise from the neighbourhood. This was a huge change from the put-downs I'd grown accustomed to. Winning became an aphrodisiac, and I became obsessed with being the best and, maybe in time, becoming the leader of my own gang.

One day I was leafing through a boxing magazine at my uncle's barbershop when I came across an ad on how to fight commando-style. I was so intrigued that I sent away for the material. About six weeks later, a package arrived in the mail. It contained eight pages of illustrations and instructions on how to use various parts of the body as lethal weapons, including the head, elbows, knees, feet, and hands. I was a little shocked at the brutal nature of the course. However, I was also fascinated by it. There were illustrations on how to gouge eyes, break kneecaps, bust ribs and noses. There were also instructions on flips, judo chops, and assorted methods of kicks to the knees and groin area, not really the stuff kids should be learning. It was a military instruction manual, and a few years later the book was pulled from the market, but for a long time my gang and I used the sheets as a handbook on street combat tactics. I kept them hidden under the floorboards of the shed in the backyard, and the only time I took them out was to practise my moves.

The fighting techniques I was learning would provide me with an edge, but I also needed more strength, size, and stamina if I intended to trade blows with the border cities' baddest dudes. To accomplish those goals, I built a set of crude weights out of concrete blocks. I worked out six days a week, strengthening my legs, shoulders, back, and the backs of my arms, the areas that generate most of the punching power. Forget all about that big biceps propaganda crap. Python arms are mostly window dressing and do little to enhance punching power. Most of the big-armed guys I knew hung on street corners with their sleeves rolled up grandstanding for the ladies, but it was mostly swagger.

When it came to fighting, if they couldn't get you with a sucker shot, it was usually game over for them!

At the end of each workout, I'd slip on a pair of my father's discarded old steel-toed boots and practise kicking techniques. They felt as though they weighed a ton, and, when I removed them after workouts, my legs would feel as light as feathers. In time, I became so proficient using the boots that I could kick more quickly than most guys could hit with their hands.

A Great Thief

CHAPTER 12

By the time I was fourteen, I was rebelling more and more against my parents, which brought endless conflict on the home front. I'd grown too big for Ma to physically discipline me; instead, when she got upset, she'd swing at me, which I found amusing. Ma was only a hundred pounds soaking wet with a hundred dollars worth of change in her pocket. When she commenced swinging, I'd just bob and weave. Eventually, she'd run out of steam and end up crying.

Like most mothers with their sons, mine refused to believe that I was really bad. Maybe a little confused but not rotten bad like the thugs I associated with. I sensed as much, which made her easy prey for my manipulative ways, and after a few words of regret from me she generally hugged and forgave me.

However, apologies work only for so long, and, if you continue to do the same stupid things over and over as I did, they begin to ring hollow. Eventually, intuition told Ma the

103

painful truth: I was heading for big trouble. She cried a lot for me in those days. After a while, I became immune to it. Her tears became just another part of my screwed-up life.

As for my father, our relationship had grown strained and distant. How many times can you let someone down before he loses faith in you? Besides playing hooky, I was getting into constant trouble with the law and shaming his good name. It wasn't supposed to be this way for the son of a preacher man. Things came to a head a few days after Christmas of 1962.

One night while the family was asleep, I broke into a cabinet in the living room where Dad kept his Christmas tip money. He'd worked the same mail route for twenty-odd years, and at Christmas the people left tips for him in their mailboxes. It was money he used to catch up on bills, maybe buy us a new mattress or some shoes. In all, he had about ninety dollars stored away. The first time I hit it, I lifted forty dollars — more than Dad made in a week.

The next morning I skipped school, shot downtown, and copped me a black mock-leather jacket and a pair of iridescent blue dress slacks. For a kid who'd been wearing hand-me-downs and secondhand clothes all his life, it felt so cool to get sharp. I'd watched the older kids dressing clean, but I'd never imagined I ever would. The thought of ripping off my father played on my mind, but the excitement of my new wardrobe dimmed my sense of guilt.

First thing I did was roll by the pool hall to do a little grandstanding. I walked in, and a couple of older dudes eyeballed me up and down, checking out the new-look kid.

"Hey, lookit here. Young-blood Jones getting with it," a guy named Bunky said, slipping me some skin. "You lookin' real sharp, baby!"

I wasn't used to compliments of that nature, and it made me swell up like a peacock. I tried to jive talk and impress him with some BS. "Yeah, thanks, my man. I got me a fine lady doing me right," I said, posing and trying to look older and cooler at the same time.

It was too early to go home, so I dropped by Big Jim's place. On weekends, Jim's was always crowded; even some of the city's police force sat in on the dice and poker games. One night I saw this cop blow his whole roll at the craps table. Instead of being upset, he just grinned and asked Jim to walk him to the side door. As they were heading down the stairs, Jim passed the cop a roll of bills. They exchanged a few pleasantries, and then the cop was on his way. Jim had a deal with him that any dough he blew at the table would be returned. It was a sweetheart deal for The Man. In return, he watched Jim's back. Pillars of the black community used to shake their heads and wonder aloud why Big Jim never got busted. Jim had the fix in pretty good.

Sometimes there'd be a couple of foxy ladies lounging on Jim's front sofa, mellowing out on wine and displaying yards of skin. It was tough for a virgin like me, whose biological urges were out of control, to handle. At first, I assumed they were somebody's squeeze. Then one night I was out in the kitchen putting empty beer bottles back into a case when I overheard this American dude whisper to Jim.

"Brother, that Cubby girl is a fine-looking piece of meat. Whatcha need for me to get with her?"

"Forty dollars, Canadian," Jim replied.

It's hard to believe now, but at that time Canadian money was actually worth more than American money. The dude dug into his kick and laid the money on Jim; then he rushed into the living room and whispered something into Cubby's ear. Cubby looked toward the kitchen, and Big Jim nodded. Then they headed upstairs to the back bedroom, which everyone called the hoochie-coo room. It was how I became aware of prostitution and realized that hookers weren't always on corners standing under streetlights.

Aside from being a big-time fence, Jim was also a major loan shark. You'd see him outside the welfare office at the first of the month. Half of Windsor's poor blacks were into Jim for money. If they didn't borrow for rent or food, they borrowed for gambling, because Big Jim was also the local numbers man.

He had a little flunky named Johnny T who chauffeured him around in a big Mercury V-8. Johnny would pull up to the curb beside the welfare office lineup, and Jim would be in the passenger seat, his shoulder hard against the door, with the window rolled down. One by one, after they got their welfare money, people would go meekly over to settle up their debts. And no one dared mess with Jim. He was a big man, going about six foot four and over 250 pounds, and he had a mean streak. He looked fat, but that was deceptive, because under that fat was hard muscle. He always spoke in a soft, low voice, and he didn't bother ordinary dudes, but if you didn't pay your debt Big Jim went looking for you. I personally saw him shake up a couple of dudes pretty bad. He was much feared in the border cities for good reason.

As I started hanging around Jim's place more — cleaning up ashtrays and fetching beer and doing other odd jobs during big card games going down — I got a good look at his setup. It wasn't like most other homes in our part of town.

Like most homes in our area, it had a smell all right, but at Jim's it was the smell of money.

Upstairs it was nicely furnished, but downstairs, in the basement, Jim was in a different world. He sent me down one time to the big locked room — which really took up the whole basement — to fetch something. He gave me the key and said, "Kid, make sure you lock up again, and bring this key right back!" I said, "Yessir." I wasn't going to mess with Jim. When I opened the door, I was blown away by what I saw. The place looked like an appliance and electronics emporium. Stacked along both walls and all across the back and even in aisles down the centre were TVs, stereos, radios, toasters. Every kind of small and portable appliance or electronic machine you could think of. All hot, and many still in their original boxes. That's when I got a true appreciation for the scale of Jim's operation.

I'd sit around Jim's place half the night listening in fascination to the pimps and thieves tell stories of whores and robberies. At first sight of dawn, I'd run home and slip through the bedroom window before Dad got up. Most of the time I couldn't get to sleep by then, so I'd just lie there and go over what I'd heard that night. I dreamed of pulling heists on my own.

My first solo theft went down in a parking lot across the street from a major department store in downtown Windsor. I spotted a pair of brass table lamps sitting in the back seat of a car. I scanned the area to see if anybody was looking. My heart was thudding. Should I, or shouldn't I? I decided to go for it, and I pulled a large, flat-nosed screwdriver out of my jacket pocket and popped the front draft window. I checked the area again. People were walking around, but no one was paying attention to me, so I reached in and unlocked the front door, snatched the lamps, and ran like hell! I don't think I'd ever moved faster in my life. I was pumped all the way home, excited about pulling my first heist. I intended to unload the lamps on Jim but figured it was best to let him know first, so I stashed them in our back shed. It was the first of many times that I'd stash hot goods in my parents' shed.

That night, after the family turned in, I crept out the window and over to Big Jim's. When I told Jim about the lamps, he nodded his approval and told me to go get them right away. I ended up making five dollars for the pair.

One Friday night, while I was heading downtown looking for something to steal, I noticed a line of luxury cars parked in front of a steam bath house: T-birds, Caddies, New Yorkers. Most of them had American plates. As I was passing by a big Lincoln, I noticed this heavyset black dude leaning over and putting something into the glove compartment. I stopped dead in my tracks. "This dude's hiding his cash," I told myself. I'd heard that when guys went into the baths they hid their money and valuables in their cars. That's what he was doing. He lifted himself up and reached into his back pocket, stooped over, and shoved something under the front seat. I knew it was his wallet. I backed up quickly and hid behind a large tree. A few seconds later, he hopped out of the car, hurried across the street, and went into the steam bath.

I popped the window, jumped into the car, and closed the door behind me to kill the interior light. I felt under the seat until I located what he had hidden. It was as I had figured — his wallet. I didn't even take the time to rummage through it.

I just shoved it into my jacket pocket and then popped the glove compartment and struck the jackpot! Inside was a gold ring with a large diamond and an expensive-looking watch. I grabbed them and booted it out of there.

I waited till I reached the shed before going through the wallet. I then discovered that I was fifty-five dollars richer. I dumped the wallet into a sewer on the way to Jim's, where I unloaded the ring and watch for another thirty-five bucks. I was riding on a cloud that night with ninety dollars in my kick. I don't know what made me feel more gratified, the money or Big Jim's praising me up: "Kid, you're going to be a great thief one day."

That night I reached home in the early evening, and, before entering the house, I crept into the back shed and removed my new jacket and slacks and slipped back into my old clothes. When I went into the house, Dad was relaxing in his easy chair, reading the Bible, and smoking his pipe. He glanced up and flashed a warm smile. Pangs of guilt shot through me. How could I betray this decent man?

Nevertheless, a few weeks later, I betrayed him again when I slipped back into his tip stash and swung with the remaining fifty dollars. This time I shot across to Detroit and got me my first conk job at the barber school on Brush Avenue. Conk jobs were popular in those days with blacks who wanted their hair straight and slicked back, like Chuck Berry or Little Richard. Some called it "marcelled" or a "fry job" because the procedure called for the barber to work in lots of burning lye and steaming water to work the kinks out. If the lye didn't scorch your scalp off, there was a good chance the steaming water would. It wasn't fun, but it sure looked cool. I also picked up a pair of shiny, patent leather loafers.

That night when I arrived home, again I slipped my new threads off and hid them in the shed, but the second I entered the house my instincts kicked in. The house was far too quiet!

"Boy! Where's my damn money!" Dad roared, his voice seething with rage.

It sent shivers through me. Dad came charging at me, swinging. I backed up a couple of steps and threw my hands up, but he waded in slapping at me with both hands.

"Where's my damn money, you thief? Where's my money?"

I tried to bob and weave like I did when Ma swung at me, but it didn't work with Dad — he was too fast, too powerful. The force of his blows sent me reeling onto the couch. I tried to run, but another blow caught me on the side of the head and stunned me. I tumbled back onto the couch. My head was spinning.

Somewhere distant I could hear the faint voices of my sisters screaming, "No, Daddy! Please, Daddy, stop!"

"Stop, Clarence, you're going to kill him!" my mother screamed as she rushed between us. She risked injury by placing herself between Dad and me.

He stormed out of the house and next door to Grandma Jones's. I noticed he had tears streaming down his face. I had angered and hurt a good and gentle person. A man who did whatever it took to provide a roof over our heads. It was wrong! Any person who steals is wrong, but when you rip off your own parents you lose something else — self-respect. That incident haunted me for years.

Before it, Dad had never laid a hand on me. And after that, he never touched me again. In fact, he hardly even looked at me. I guess he either gave up on me or just figured it wouldn't do any good to punish me. If that was the case, then he was right. I'd lost all fear of punishment.

Things really changed in our house after that night. Dad and Ma kept their money on them at all times. Whenever I was around, Ma kept her purse close to her, and Dad began to sleep on his wallet. Losing their trust was a sinking blow to my self-esteem. I felt like an outcast in my own family, but I was too angry at the world to care. I despised living in that old rat-infested, cramped-up house. I was angry about sleeping on stinking, rotted mattresses. Angry with my parents for being poor and still having so many kids. Angry with the kids who constantly taunted me with racial slurs and about my body odour. I was tired of smelling like stale urine and wearing secondhand clothes and hand-me-downs. I was angry with my teachers for not being able to understand my problems. But most of all, I was full of self-loathing. The kind that fills the mind and the heart with pain and turns you against society.

School had become a drag, and church was for fools. I was craving the streets like an addict craves his drug. The lure was like a supernatural force that had invaded my mind and taken control of me. Grandma Jones said the Devil was seducing me. I guess she was right.

In 1961, I dropped out of school for good. I'd had it with the system. I wasn't going anywhere in school, and I wasn't allowed to defend myself against the racist attacks that didn't stop. I was fifteen and still only in grade four because I'd been held back so many times, but the trouble I was getting into was starting to escalate. Following yet another school-yard fight, I refused to allow the teacher to strap me. So I was suspended. I simply decided not to return.

The law required you to be sixteen to quit school without the permission of your parents. However, things were going so badly both at school and at home that my father gladly signed my release papers with the understanding that I'd look for a job. Needless to say, with an educational status the equivalent of grade four, no job offers materialized, but I had no intention of getting a job anyway. I was making pretty good money my own way.

My life then became that of a full-time street punk.

I began sleeping all day, hanging around the streets most of the night, floating around the periphery of the criminal world. My newfound aggression was becoming like protective emotional armour.

During that year, I had repeated confrontations with the law, and I spent some time in detention after I was arrested for rolling drunks. I'd look for someone off balance from booze, sneak up on him, whack him with my homemade blackjack, and pull the money from his pockets. If he resisted, I'd throw a few punches to take the fight out of him.

After I served a few months, my parents decided that maybe I needed a change of scenery, so I moved across the border and took up more or less permanent residence with my Aunt Ida in the Brewster Projects. Aside from mostly hanging out on the street, I began doing a bit of informal singing in teen clubs, and I was still getting into a lot of fights. I decided to become either a singer or a boxer, and I figured the move to Motown might present me with more career opportunities.

Detroit did present more opportunities — just not in the career choices I had in mind.

Smokers

I had been hearing about "smokers" for years — they were legendary in the black communities — but I had no idea that I was going to be in the middle of one until I found myself half naked and surrounded by strangers screaming for my blood.

It began one Saturday afternoon when the phone rang at Ida's, and I heard my aunt say "What you want with him, boy?" with that mixture of suspicion and disapproval she reserved for certain of my friends. I knew it had to be my main man, TC, so I grabbed up the phone.

I'd pulled a lot of heists with TC; we'd covered each other's back for years. I hadn't heard from him for a while, and I knew Ida hoped I had upgraded my choice of street associates. She considered TC a bad influence. The truth was TC hadn't called only because he was serving a ninety-day stretch for bootlegging. But he was now free, and he'd got his hands on some quick money, and he wanted to celebrate his release.

113

So on a hot Saturday evening in August, at about eight o'clock, I found myself hanging out on the sidewalk in front of the Greystone Ballroom on Woodward Avenue, waiting for TC to show. The Greystone was the hottest teen joint in Detroit, and I was broke, busted, disgusted, and couldn't be trusted, but I couldn't let all that show. I was trying my best to look cool while critically appraising the passing female population.

While I wasn't crazy about some of the house rules at Aunt Ida's, I loved living in Detroit. I loved the music, I loved the vibrant feeling on the street. Good music, good food, and good times were everywhere. But you always had to keep your head up. Motor City had the dubious reputation as the most violent city in America. Hanging in front of the Greystone meant that I was open game for rival gangs. These were violent times, and there was always somebody looking for a mark to lay his hurt on. And if you weren't dodging opposing gang members with chips on their shoulders, you had to watch out for Detroit's finest, dudes with even bigger chips on their shoulders plus badges that gave them licence to beat on whomever they wanted.

Friends cruising past would call out, "Hey, what's happenin', my man!"

My response was always the same: "Hey, baby, ain't nuthin' shakin' but the bacon."

TC finally showed. "Hey, my man," he said, and we embraced and did our high-five ritual.

Right off I noticed three unusual things about his deportment. First, TC was all decked out in a fancy — spell that *ex*-p-e-n-s-i-v-e — blue mohair suit and shiny new loafers, and his hair wasn't its usual kinky self but a wavy and "marcelled" job. I had to admit TC was looking gooood! He'd been out of jail only a few days, and already he was decked out in new duds and a new hairdo. There had to be a story there.

The second thing I noticed was that he had a swelled-up shiner under his right eye. That had to be another story. I said, "Hey, man, who kicked your sorry ass?"

TC shot me his cocky sneer and growled, "Bro, *nobody* kicks TC's ass!"

Then, before I could quiz him about the duds and the shiner, he pulled out a roll of large-calibre bills — tens and twenties — that would have choked Godzilla. Wha-a-a-a-! My eyes popped. Now that had to be a *big* story!

"I got me these babies last night. My first week out, and I made two bills already."

"Two bills!" Two hundred dollars was not chump change — it was a lot of money for that time! The sight of that bankroll blew my broke-ass mind. An Abe Lincoln (a U.S. five-dollar bill) was still a big deal to me.

Where had this money come from? But TC was playing coy. He wouldn't tell me straight off. So I set in to badgering at him, but TC was tight-lipped. I knew that whatever it was it had to be big-time! I kept at him. I stuck to him like a fly on a horse's rump. From the moment he rose at the crack of noon until he retired in the wee hours of the morning, I was there, leaning on him to crack. I wanted *in*.

For a long time, he kept laying the same old story on me. "I'm working on it for you, man," he'd say.

I knew that, if I stayed tightly on his case, sooner or later he'd give up what I wanted: the key to all that cash. By mid-week, he cracked.

"Okay," he finally said. "Bro, do you *really* want in?"

I said, "Do black folks party in Harlem?"

"Okay. Meet me at Grand River and Hudson tomorrow night. And be ready to *go*."

I couldn't sleep that night. Be ready to "go" at what?

The next night TC met me at the corner. He pulled up with his cousin Trooper behind the wheel of Trooper's old '48 Chevy flat top. TC was in the front passenger seat. He said, "Hop in, Bro."

I hopped in the back.

Trooper was another member of our crew. He peeled away, and I settled back to ponder exactly what was going on. They had made such a big secret of it that I had no idea what we were headed to, but I had a bad feeling about it. Both TC and Trooper weren't their usual loud selves. TC always had a macho swagger about him, and Trooper was a loudmouthed party dude who couldn't whip cream but would slice you like cheese with a blade. I assumed, from their subdued manner, that we were heading either for a big B-and-E job or for some gang trouble. Before trouble, TC always became quiet and sullen, tensing up for what was to come, like prefight nerves.

Trooper headed east, out of Detroit, through the Windsor tunnel, and across town. Nobody spoke. About twenty miles out of Windsor, we turned north off the highway, down a concession road. Finally, I couldn't take the tension, the quiet, and the uncertainty anymore.

"Look, what's the deal?" I demanded.

They both kept their eyes straight ahead and ignored me.

I asked again.

TC turned slowly to give me a meaningful look. "It's time to get down, brother. We going to kick ass tonight."

That was it. That was all he'd say. So it *was* gang business. I began to brace myself mentally.

Trooper turned onto a gravel back road, and dust began to swirl behind us. I looked out the side window with a tightening feeling in my gut. Shadows of trees flickered across the passenger window of the car like spectral images, and I thought, "Damn, I'm sick of this violence crap. Brother hurting brother. For what?" I'd seen too many guys walk away from gang rumbles with severe physical damage. *If* they could walk at all. Gut sliced. Forearm sliced. Face sliced. Clubbed. Kicked. Some got carried away or departed by ambulance. In the past year, a dozen friends of ours had been seriously injured in gang battles, several not surviving their injuries. The last thing I wanted to be doing was heading toward another gang showdown. I was getting tired of it. Besides, I wondered how *that* was going to turn into cash.

In my pocket was the spring-loaded switchblade that I carried in those days. I was thumbing the smoothly polished handle, and the sick feeling in the pit of my stomach was growing. While I had to act as tough as the rest of the street crowd I hung with — and I was tougher than most of them in many ways — I still couldn't come to terms with a cold steel blade slicing into someone's soft flesh. It gave me the creeps to even think about it, and I had never used a blade on anyone. I truly doubted that I could, even if I got backed into a corner. I was good with my hands, as a boxer, and I'd rely on my boxing skills if it came down to it. But these were not the kinds of thoughts you shared with your gang associates. You had to make them think that you were as crazy and as bad as they were. It was the only way to get respect.

Also, I felt I was betraying my father — yet again. Dad

despised anyone who carried weapons. I used to laugh behind his back and think how easy it was for him, so big and so strong, to sneer at weapons. Nobody messed with Pops, and he was a good man whom I agreed with — mostly. I just couldn't get with him on this business about how only a coward carries a weapon. Some of the toughest cats I knew carried weapons, usually for their own protection, because everyone around them did also.

After about an hour of driving, we were well into the countryside, passing through a little Ontario town called Colchester, a summer resort located beside a small inland lake with an oldtime music band shell. It was popular in summer, especially with border city blacks, for bringing in big-name groups. I had seen the Drifters and a few other big acts there. I thought maybe the rumble was going to be at the pavilion. There had been a lot of clashes of late between Windsor and Detroit border gangs. But I had to be careful because, while I was hanging in Detroit a lot, I was still a Windsor guy, so I couldn't afford to get my loyalties crossed up.

It grew dark, and we pulled onto an even smaller gravel road. Just ahead, parked cars lined both sides of this two-lane country road, and we turned onto a long dirt driveway, also lined with cars parked on the grass at every crazy angle. We found a spot to pull in. Cars were also parked helter-skelter all over the lawn and in the fields. There must have been fifty or more vehicles at this place. Something big was going down there.

I remember the fresh smell of farm fields and the sound of crickets as we stepped out. Then the smells and sounds of the country were quickly replaced by the smells, sights, and sounds of the scene. In the centre of the field was a farm with an old, two-storey, wood-frame farmhouse in which every window and door was brightly lit. As we approached, I noticed a big fire in a pit casting shadows of people moving around it. Speakers were set up on the front lawn blasting music across the property. I remember the song that was blaring as we walked up the drive: Lloyd Price's version of "Stagger Lee." People were dancing inside the house and all around the yard. Smoke and the tangy smell of roasting meats from the fire pit — burgers, hot dogs, chicken, and ribs slathered in special sauces — floated over the scene. People were selling food at little stands set up on the lawn near the fire.

What the hell was *this*? This wasn't a gang rumble. Everyone was festive. It was some sort of huge *party*.

Then TC turned, shot me one of his sly grins, and said, "Are you ready, baby?" Before I could even answer, he hollered, "Tonight's the *night*! It's smoker time, baby! You gonna get you some."

And he and Trooper both high-fived me.

Right away my heart began to pound.

"Now? A smoker? Here? Who do I fight? Do we all fight? Where do we fight? . . ." My heart was racing.

There on the grass under the moonlight TC gave me the abbreviated version of what to expect as we walked toward the scene. It was how he'd made so much quick money out of jail, which is where he'd learned about them. Smokers were illegal and informal boxing matches with heavy side-betting action that took place in a number of northern U.S. states and just across the border into Canada, like there, outside Windsor. They could take place anywhere from rural farm settings, like that place, to abandoned warehouses in downtown Detroit or Cleveland. They were kept hush-hush, not only because they were illegal, but also because they attracted so many underworld players, and nobody wanted a raid coming down.

TC said, "Just stick with me, and do *exactly* what I tell you. I've cleared it with the people here, but you gotta handle yourself right."

I was relieved to learn that it wasn't a gang confrontation, but my adrenaline was pumping as though I'd lift straight off the ground — it was show time, and I was going to be centre stage. I was excited but nervous. TC walked me around a bit to level me out after hitting me with the news. Many of the licence plates, I noticed as we walked, were from outside Ontario: Michigan, Ohio, Illinois, Pennsylvania, even New York. This was a big event, obviously well publicized, not publicly in newspapers but through the underworld grapevine. My first tip-off to the big-money side of these things was the number of new Cadillacs and Lincolns I saw, the cars of choice of pimps, hustlers, and loan sharks. There were also lots of late-model Buicks and Oldsmobiles, big Detroit-built cars, all of which cost a lot of money in those days. You never saw European or Japanese cars then. So this was a well-heeled crowd with lots of cash to spread around.

The barbecue was a deep pit dug in the earth with brick sides and a massive iron grate laid across it. It smelled delicious, but I had no appetite. Just up the lawn from the pit were large galvanized tubs packed with ice and beer, also for sale. I also didn't have a desire to drink. Even as a kid, I knew that booze slows the metabolism, the brain, and the reflexes. If you're going to fight, you need every fraction of a second.

And I counted on speed. I wasn't hefty enough to count on punching power. I knew that I'd need every resource I had to get through that night. I'd been hounding TC for a week, so there was no backing out now.

A grey, weathered barn sat on a small rise behind the house. Light from inside was spraying from between the vertical barn boards, shooting shards of light into the darkness. I knew that inside were the players and the big shots. I followed TC up the earthen ramp to the wide-open barn doors.

Inside, in a blue haze of smoke, it was bright, loud, and jumping with players of all kinds — blacks, whites, Italians, Latinos. The men were decked for a night out, in suits, like going to the real fights, and the women wore slinky evening dresses that showed lots of cleavage. I learned that not only rounders and players but also "respectable people" — politicians, businessmen, off-duty policemen — attended these events. The place was packed, and the scent of stogies, cigarettes, and perfume — mingled with hay and straw — filled the air.

A makeshift ring had been thrown up: four poles nailed into the plank flooring with two strands of thick hemp rope thrown around, making a crude ring eighteen by eighteen, about the size of a pro ring. There were hay bales everywhere and straw all over the floor. A card game was going on at a picnic table in one corner. Seven or eight guys were playing stud poker, and a group of onlookers were standing around, drinking, and kibitzing. Other tables were set up for craps.

As we entered, some young guys standing over in the corner turned and eyeballed me, sizing me up. They were my age, and young guys didn't hang with older guys, so I knew I'd be fighting one of these dudes, and they knew they'd be fighting me. We were there for only one reason: to provide some entertainment for the big shooters. I knew that the guys eyeing me were from Detroit because they had the telltale signs of the Detroit streets: battered noses and scars. One had a long, jagged scar running from his eye to his cheek. You could see he'd been sliced with a razor. These were young, bad dudes but I felt a surge of confidence. When it came to physical play, I was on solid ground. In those days, I was doing ninety push-ups at a time three times a day, working out with my crude dumbbells, and working on a heavy bag in the back shed — an old burlap sack packed solid with rags.

Also, my father had taught me the value of a left jab. He used to say, "A guy comes at you, slam that jab up. Snap it out and bring it right back like you're touching a hot brick. Bust his nose, and you got a guy who can't see straight." I had practised for hours and got lightning fast with the jab.

I felt that I was ready for anything.

CHAPTER 14

Living Large

Smokers were so informal that the combatants didn't dress in boxing shorts and lace-up boots. Nor did they tape their hands, which is essential in boxing to prevent hand damage. It was "go as you are." I was still in a crew-neck T-shirt and a pair of Levi's held up by a belt made of rope. I felt like a black Huck Finn. I felt like that most of my boyhood. When it came to clothes, I often couldn't be too choosy about size and fit, of course, because I'd picked them off a line on a midnight shopping excursion.

A big black dude named Sampson played a prominent role in smokers in the Windsor area. I knew Sampson from seeing him around Big Jim's, and TC took me over to the card game to speak to him about clearing me in.

"Howerya doin', Jonesie, you gettin' in on the action tonight?"

I nodded, wild-eyed.

He glanced in the direction of my opponent. "This kid

can go. I seen him. Got good hands. You got a fight on your hands tonight, Jonesie."

That just put me more on edge.

He offered us a beer, which TC and Trooper took but which I again declined.

We watched the card game for a while, and I noticed that every time money went into the pot, even before the bets were placed, Sampson reached in and took his cut out of the money in the centre. His cut came right off the top, no risk and no questions asked.

Then it was time for the smokers. There were three before mine. I watched in fascination. The more the crowd yelled, the more excited I got about my turn. It was like performing, and I found myself looking forward to it.

Finally, my turn came. I took off my shirt, and that was it for prefight prep. They brought in these beat-up old gloves that might have been padded when they were new, but they'd been through about a thousand sparring rounds, and they were now well broken down. These fights, of course, were unsanctioned as far as any boxing body went. You were on your own, and there were only a few rules: you couldn't kick or head-butt, you had to use your hands, but you *could* use your elbows.

Serving as the referee was one of the overweight, out-of-shape organizers. He came into the ring and introduced the boxers, playing it up real big, and there I was, suddenly under the lights and dancing around to loosen up. Muhammad Ali — fighting as Cassius Clay in those days — was just becoming big then, though he wasn't yet champion, and I'd been following his career since he'd turned pro. So I was dancing around limbering up just like Ali: shaking my legs, shaking my arms, shaking my head, looking generally loose and cool all over. Side-bet activity was going on all around the barn, and I knew that if I won I'd not only get the thirty-dollar prize but also pick up more in tips from the gamblers. High rollers called out to me: "Hey, kid, you win, and I'll take care of you."

I was intro'd as Kid Lightning, and though I tried to look cool I was shaking inside. I'd been in a lot of street scraps and a lot of sparring sessions but never in a ring before an unruly crowd. The barn was full to the rafters. People were well into the booze, the eating was done, the side of beef was gone from the barbecue, and now they wanted to see some action. I'd heard about people being so scared that they crapped or pissed themselves, but I'd never understood it before. Now I did! I was so nervous I thought I'd have a bowel movement right there in centre ring.

I was trying to distract myself by concentrating on the kid opposite me. A mean-looking kid. He had this short, kinky hair and a thick neck and wide shoulders. He was about an inch shorter than I was, stocky, and well developed. And he had a long, ugly scar on his elbow from some knife or razor wound. He wore a tight tank top, which accentuated his bulging muscles. He might have been twenty, a big age advantage on me.

One thing I always did was lock eyes with my opponents; doing so unsettles them. I learned that watching Sonny Liston, master of the evil glare. And I was bouncing up and down, psyching myself up, and trying to psyche him out. When it came to boxing, unless the guy was a big-time amateur boxer, he wasn't going to beat me. Also, by then I was six foot and about 165 pounds, a middleweight.

After the introductions, an old guy seated at ringside on a stool whacked a cowbell with a hammer to start the bout, and out we charged. When I got to centre ring, my man was flailing away, throwing punches with both hands, trying to hit me with anything he could, and right away I stuck in my left jab. I caught him squarely on the nose as planned, and blood started squirting right away. That was my fight plan: stick and move, stick and move.

I was in tremendous physical shape, but he was panting after just sixty seconds. He threw a dangerous shot, and all that practice in the gym came back to me like instincts: I stepped under it and threw a hard uppercut counterpunch that caught him on the ribs. You could hear him grunt as the air was sucked out of him. Then I threw an elbow into his other ribs. Then I stuck my foot behind his, put the palm of my glove under his chin, and pushed — something I'd learned street fighting. And over he went. He fell back hard and only staggered up slowly. He was bleeding badly, blood running down his face onto his chest.

The roar of that crowd packed into that barn felt sooo good. They were cheering for *me*! Man, it turned me right on.

They stopped the fight because the guy was bleeding badly, his eye was swollen shut, and his wind was shot. It had lasted only five minutes, but everyone cheered and held my hand up like I'd won the Olympic Gold.

That was my first smoker, but after that night I was hooked. Man, I loved the feeling of victory in the ring!

There were six or seven fights after mine. One guy, an older, experienced heavyweight from Cleveland called Hammer, walked away with three hundred bucks between his purse and tips thrown his way. In 1961, that was ten times

the average weekly wage. Muhammad Ali, in his second pro
fight the year before, had won a purse of only two hundred.
So smokers rivalled legitimate boxing for the money that
could be made.

Smokers earned me spending money through many of
my teenage years. Still, it wasn't the easiest way to make
dough. They took a heavy toll on my hands. My fists were
too brittle for banging on hard heads.

About that time, I also came face to face with the dude
George Foreman would later call "the toughest man on the
planet." I walked into the Big D one day and heard all this
heavy thudding going on over in the heavy-bag corner, and
there was a small crowd of people gathered around watching. So I peeped a look, and there was this monster of a
white dude with dark, closely cut hair, and he was banging
the poor bag to bits. I mean the power was startling. His
back was facing me, and all I could see were these wide,
muscled shoulders and this massive neck, which belonged to
George Chuvalo, the Canadian heavyweight champ.

George was about twenty-five then, and he had moved to
Detroit to train at the Big D with Teddy McWhorters. Teddy
introduced us, and George and I became good friends that
day, even though he was older, because he could tell I really
knew my fight stuff, thanks to my dad. What was so cool
about George was that, in those days, he was the only white
guy who worked out at the Big D, but all the brothers liked
and respected him right away. Not that anybody was frightened of him — these were guys who came from bad-ass
'hoods themselves, so they didn't care about how tough a
guy was — but they accepted George because he fit in so

well. He loved soul food, Jackie Wilson, Marvin Gaye, R&B music, and the whole downtown Detroit black scene. He lived downtown, he ate downtown, and his was one of the few white faces you'd see down there every day.

I was also becoming active then in the Golden Gloves program through the Police Athletic Club of Windsor. In my first Golden Gloves fight the year before, at age fourteen, I won the Windsor novice title. In later years, I went on to win welterweight, middleweight, and light-heavyweight Golden Gloves titles. So Golden Gloves boxing was something I did off and on for almost twenty years.

One night after a smoker, a group of us were lounging around my sister Rose's crib in Detroit. I was nursing a pair of swollen hands compliments of two smokers in one night. While I was sitting there in pain, I began to wonder out loud how much money the promoters were pulling in. There was admission, booze, food, and side bets. Had to be a few thousand dollars, I thought. And it was falling into the manicured paws of soft-bellied street hustlers. Got me to thinking, "I'm a damn fool to let someone get rich off my blood, sweat, and pain."

"Man!" I said, "we should be doing our own promotion."

Top Cat agreed. "Yeah, but where we gonna get the start-up capital?"

Enter a street player named Bumps.

Bumps ran an illegal, after-hours joint on the west side of Detroit. His operation was much bigger than Big Jim's in Windsor. Besides bootlegging, fencing hot goods, and loan sharking, Bumps ran monster poker games. His games attracted some of the Motor City's biggest players and personalities, prime-time players from the music and sports worlds, and some were into Bumps for thousands of dollars.

He'd got his nickname because his face was a mass of boils and pimples. By his own admission, he was so ugly he had to sneak up on a glass of water. And his breath stank so bad he could knock you over with a good yawn. Bumps may have been an ugly dude, but nobody said it to his face. He was street bad and would bust a cap in you quicker than heaven got the news. But what I really admired about Bumps was the fact that he never allowed his lack of looks to cramp his style. He was one smooth-talking dude. Sometimes, when we were sitting around, Bumps would give lessons on how to pull the ladies. I never saw him hit the clubs without a fox on each arm.

One afternoon Bumps called TC and me to do some collecting on a couple of delinquent loans. We did this on occasion to raise some quick cash, but I really hated collecting these debts. It meant running all over the city tracking down poor suckers to shake them down. Most of them were just poor street hustlers with big gambling problems and no money — losers always looking for the jackpot. When we did catch up with them, generally they'd whine like babies and give us all kinds of sob stories. I'm a sucker for sob stories, so being a collector wasn't my thing. In fact, on many occasions, I let them slide.

One day while we were settling up with Bumps for some collection we had done, he asked how we'd fared at the last smoker. I told him how tired I was of somebody else ending up with most of the money, while we fighters took home the hurt.

"We can promote our own fights," Top Cat told him. "We just need the money to get it going."

"Hold on, brother!" Bumps said excitedly. You could tell we had pushed the right button. His big eyes got that greedy glare. "How much money you need?"

Over the next few hours, we worked out a plan. He'd provide funds for the booze, food, and cash prizes for the fighters. Our end was to promote the event, set up the fights, and act as security. Bumps would get his investment back, and we'd split the rest fifty-fifty.

The first couple of events went off without a hitch, and we took in some pretty good dough. Top Cat and I were living large and moving up in the game. We were now purchasing our clothes from stores in the heart of downtown Detroit, upscale men's shops like Todd's and Sherman's, where all the players and high street rollers went to get clean. We bought some boss threads, including suits, ties, and silk shirts. We also copped a couple of Chicago-style gangster hats. Thought we were big-time players! Even got to thinking about moving into an uptown penthouse apartment.

Then the good times came crashing down.

Our third smoker was held north of Detroit, in Flint, in a beat-up old barn. It turned out to be our most prosperous promotion to date. The place was packed. The thing I liked most about it was that Top Cat and I didn't have to do the fighting anymore. We were now the promoters! Our end had been about eight bills apiece from each of the first two events, plus we made some solid bread placing side bets, which brought us in another grand. We also got a piece of the action from the poker games. Man, it was good!

Too good! Somebody got envious and gave us up to the cops.

About eleven o'clock, we were in full swing, and everything was percolating when, about halfway through the fights, it came down on us. Out of nowhere, the police stormed that old barn like the marines. At the time, Top Cat and Bumps were at the front door collecting admission. When the Man came busting in with guns drawn, it was game over for them; they didn't even get a chance to run.

I was near the back of the barn preparing a couple of fighters, and there was already a fight going on, so the place was so noisy you could hardly hear yourself talk, and I wasn't even aware of what was going down until a couple of the fighters came rushing back shouting "Police!" I looked around, and everywhere were uniforms and people scattering for the exits. The cops were yelling out orders to get down on the floor and were herding people toward the middle of the building. All kinds of scuffles were breaking out as people tried to escape.

I tried to spot Top Cat, but in all the turmoil it was impossible. I knew I had to get the hell out of there! If they got hold of me, it was back to jail for me.

I searched frantically for an escape route. The only exit I could see was at the front of the building. But to risk it would have been fool's play. I'd noticed earlier, as we were driving in, a grove of trees about fifty yards from the barn. There were also acres of cornfields, and if I could somehow reach that area I'd be able to escape. I crawled on hands and knees to the wall and felt the wood. It was old, soft, and rotted. I lay on my back and kicked hard with both feet. The boards gave way, and I slipped through the hole and headed for the woods.

I spent the night in the trees, watching the cops hustling people into paddy wagons. The next morning I hitched a ride into Flint, thinking I was free and clear. But when I called my sister Rose from a phone booth and asked her to pick me up, she was mad as hell.

"Two cops just been here looking for you," she snapped. "Every time you get your ass in trouble, damn cops come out here hassling me about you!"

I cooled her down so she could explain what had happened. She told me they wanted to question me about an incident that had happened last night. I knew then that somebody had given up my name. The heat was on, and once again I had to split the Motor City. The cops may have told my sister they merely wanted to question me, but I knew what they really wanted — to lock me up.

When I made it to Rose's, she told me that Top Cat's mother had called to tell her that he'd been charged with bootlegging and carrying a weapon — a gun. He'd just gotten out of the joint a few months earlier and was supposed to be on good behaviour, so I knew he was going to get another stretch. There was nothing I could do. I loved the dude, he'd been my main man for years, but I'd warned him that packing guns was out. I wished he'd taken my advice.

At two o'clock, Rose dropped me at my parents' house in Windsor, and by three-thirty I was on the Greyhound to Toronto.

CHAPTER 15

New Business Development

My retreat to Toronto lasted only a few months that time. I hooked up with some friends for a while, but it wasn't long before I was back in Windsor.

I was now getting into fistfights on an almost daily basis. Word spread in our turf that, if you messed with any of the Mercer Street Boys, you had to deal with all of us. That word also reached my parents. For them, that was enough to call for desperate measures. They shipped me off to spend the summer with my aunt and uncle on their sharecropper's farm outside Winston-Salem, North Carolina.

It was quite an eye-opener!

After being used to the insistent but often behind-your-back racism of the north, Winston-Salem was my first encounter with down-south, in-your-face segregation. The first thing I noticed was that, no matter how old black folks were, whites continued to call them "boy." This was the south before the civil rights movement: "no coloreds here" and "no colored there" and all that back-of-the-bus stuff was ingrained and routine. I began to see that, in spite of the racial problems blacks faced up north, conditions were actually less severe than in the southern states.

I wasn't there a month when I got into a fight with a white kid who called my cousin Toby a nigger. To southern blacks, being insulted was an everyday thing. Most brothers just turned the other cheek, but I was sick and tired of turning the other cheek only to get that one slapped too. I beat the kid up good. When we got back to the farm, my cousins bragged about my feat to my uncle. What did my uncle do? He took off his belt and whipped *me*. I couldn't believe it!

The next day I was put on the bus back to Detroit.

What I didn't realize was that I was not a "great defender" to my uncle and cousins; rather, I had brought the real threat of retribution to their small farm. The Klan was still active then, and black folks were still being lynched in southern states for less than what I had done.

After a few months in Detroit, I moved back to Windsor and me and some other guys formed a doo-wop group called The Galahads. We started playing small parties and clubs and ended up selling out Windsor's Palace Theatre one night. Music was looking like it might take over from boxing, street fighting, and thieving as my main pursuit.

My main thing was to get clean on weekends and slip back across the border into Detroit. First we'd hit 12th Street, drop by the Chit Chat Lounge to get a drink or two, and then we'd hit the Gold Room of the Twenty Grand, the cream of Detroit's black show bars. *The* most authentic R&B joint on the face of the Earth. But it was more than the talent that made the Twenty Grand a hot place. The crowd was every bit as entertaining as the acts on stage. 'Specially Saturday nights. Players' night out! The time when street royalty made the scene: hustlers, loan sharks, bookies, pimps, hookers, actors, businessmen, boxers, entertainers, underworld figures, all mingling together, strutting their stuff like the CBS peacock. If you weren't stylin' and profilin' in the right threads, the ladies would sound on you. They'd say, "Get out of my face, you boag-ass, country-lookin' fool," dismissing any dude whose apparel wasn't up to their standards. Sharkskin and mohair suits, Stetson hats, and needle-toe shoes were the happening things.

So were slicked-back hairdos. All the players and all the wannabes had a "do." We'd hit the barber school over on Brush Street because it was a few dollars cheaper than the pros. Most of the guys at the barber school knew what they were doing, but sometimes you'd suffer the misfortune of having a rookie work on you.

One time this novice was giving me a conk job, and he kept getting phone calls from his lady. So he'd go to the back of the shop and leave me sitting and squirming while he was running game to his lady. I tried to be cool, but my scalp was on fire. It hurt so bad there were tears in my eyes. Finally, I hollered at him, "Hey, brother! I'm frying up! Get this shit out of my hair!" By the time he got it washed out, half my hair was also down the drain. I tripped out, snatched his ass, and was about to do him in when the owner saved him. He cooled me out with twenty dollars. I had to wear a cap for a couple of months just to hide the scabs. A whole lot of us nappy-headed brothers celebrated when the Afro trend arrived — no more of them red-hot fry jobs.

The Galahads entered a talent contest at Windsor's Jackson Park, and we were the first Canadian act ever to take place first. Three unknown girls from Detroit, then calling themselves the Primettes, won the female category, but they came in second overall to us. Two years later the Primettes — Diana Ross and her childhood friends, Flo Ballard and Mary Wilson, now under Barry Gordy's management — became the Supremes, and the rest is history. After our win in the talent contest, The Galahads headlined the Greystone Ballroom, and we opened the Michigan State Fair for the Spinners. We were on our way, right behind Diana and her Primettes . . . or so I thought!

Then two of our four members were charged and convicted of grand theft auto and sent upstate for twenty-four months less a day, and our lead singer, Buck, died shortly after in a car crash, and The Galahads disbanded as quickly as we had started. That setback just embittered me even more.

I went back to my old thieving ways.

By 1964, the Mercer Street Boys had evolved into the Mobsters. Ducky, Vampire, and Greasy got busted trying to hold up a bank in Pontiac, Michigan, and they ended up doing major time in the Jackson pen. Not long afterward, my cousin Sonny was shot to death in a feud over a woman.

Then, just a few days before Christmas, my cousin Leroy was murdered just off 12th Street in Detroit. He'd gone downtown with some money in his pocket to buy a Christmas present for his girlfriend. Police said he'd been beaten with a blunt object — likely a bat — and his murder was never solved. It became just another in a long list of mindless, unsolved murders in Motor City that year. It was a difficult time for our family. Leroy and I were like brothers, but his death was especially tough on my mother, who had raised him after his mom, Mary, my mom's youngest sister, had died when Leroy was very young. Ma mourned Leroy's loss for years.

Sonny's and Leroy's deaths should have driven me away from street life; instead, they were just two more incidents that drove me to the streets even more as the only place I thought I had any control over my destiny, as bleak as that was.

Most of the remaining members of the gang ended up in either jail or reform school. With our ranks thinning fast, Top Cat — back out of jail — became president of the Mobsters, and I became vice president. I was also in charge of "new business development." Most of our efforts continued to be concentrated on burglaries, but we moved up from houses to businesses and factories, which proved to be a great deal more lucrative. Being the most knowledgeable in the burglaries department, I was in charge of blueprinting our heists. A lot of my information came from Big Jim and a couple of other fences. Back then alarm and surveillance systems weren't as advanced as they are today, so it wasn't difficult to break in. Most places we hit had systems that were crude by today's standards, usually just bars across doors and windows.

I was also in charge of moving the merchandise. Underworld people are inherently suspicious, so everything must be done in a discreet manner, which is understandable; one slip equals big jail time. I sold our goods to three major fences, but Big Jim always got first crack.

One night at the Greystone, frequented by members of various gangs and always full of that volatile mix of testosterone and simmering grudges, I was trying hard to get next to a foxy lady named Tina. We were slow-dancing and necking up a storm when Top Cat came over and yanked me off the dance floor to rush to our buddy Chico's aid.

Some dudes had attacked Chico, and when we found them I was once again in the middle of a vicious gang rumble. Before it was over, some crazy dude had pulled a straight razor and sliced me deeply across my right wrist. There was blood spurting all over the place. My new red silk shirt and pants got soaked in my own blood. They had to rush me downtown to the hospital, and I ended up with a dozen stitches.

Not long afterward, a couple of kids from our turf were beaten up by a group of white guys during a street dance. Kenny, one of our guys, made the mistake of asking some white guy's girl for a dance, and the dude threw a sucker shot that broke Kenny's jaw. Another kid was knocked down and repeatedly kicked and suffered a concussion. They were foolish for going into the area alone, but the most disturbing aspect of the incident was that, while a dozen guys beat up two, hundreds of people witnessed the affair, and not one intervened on their behalf. Nor did anyone attempt to call the police.

It was incumbent on me as a senior member of the Mobsters to lead the revenge brigade. Word filtered back to us that the guys who'd done it were part of a west-end group called the Lansbury Lancers. I wasn't surprised. I was familiar with some of them from my school days, and I knew that they were some tough, mean, and prejudiced white kids.

Word was the guy who had suckered Kenny was their leader, a guy named Psycho. He was a crazy ass, which was how he'd got tagged with the name.

We planned our revenge for the Labour Day weekend fair at the Windsor Fairgrounds. It was an event that ran three days and attracted big crowds, and in the past it had been marred by fights between various gang factions. Besides the fights, there was always a lot of vandalism, so the grounds would be crawling with cops and security, which ruled out a confrontation on the fairgrounds itself. We wondered how to get at them when Mario, an Italian friend of mine, informed us that Psycho drove a 1956 silver Pontiac. That's when I got an idea.

Psycho would have to park in the vacant meadow across the street from the fairgrounds used as a temporary parking facility. The pathway to the fairgrounds was lined with dense bushes and oak and willow trees, their lower limbs spreading across the narrow path. It was a perfect spot for an ambush.

Earlier that summer I'd seen a movie in which the Seminole Indians were being hounded by U.S. cavalry into the Florida swamps. Although the Seminoles were badly outnumbered, they outsmarted the soldiers by luring them deeper into the swamp, and, as they passed, the Seminoles jumped from the trees and attacked them. This was my plan.

That Saturday night, from our places in the limbs of the trees, we watched the silver Pontiac cruise into the parking lot. We watched Psycho and his buddies hop out and swagger along the pathway in all their macho glory. There were five of us in the trees and close to another dozen among the shrubs and bushes. As they passed by the trees, we jumped down on them like screaming eagles.

Psycho jumped back a few steps and squinted, trying to figure us out. "We don't want no trouble with you guys," he hollered.

"Right! Remember those two black kids you and your chickenshit gang beat up on a few weeks back?" I said. "They weren't looking for any trouble either."

He had a sort of stunned expression, but he didn't respond. He had a reputation for being a monster in a street fight, and reputations can be intimidating. I've seen guys freeze after hearing how bad another dude is, but I'd been through too many smokers and street fights by then to sweat over some punk whose game was ganging kids.

It's amazing how passive most wannabe gangsters are when you cut them away from the pack. That's exactly what we did. Psycho's guys split, and we blocked Psycho, so he was on his own. He turned out to be more chicken than a dozen Kentucky Fried outlets. He and I got it on — one on one — and I smoked him in less than a minute. It felt good. After that, the black kids were pretty much left alone downtown.

Shortly after that incident, I had my closest brush yet with major time in the big house. The deal came through Bumps. . . .

Sometimes, after a big jewellery heist, I'd smuggle the merchandise over to Bumps and peddle it to his patrons. Top Cat and I would stroll in, unload a sports bag full of watches and rings, and then sit in on a game of cards or shoot some craps. A few days later we'd head back to Windsor and plan our next heist.

One afternoon Bumps invited us to the Chit Chat Lounge, told us that he had a big business deal going down, that we could pull a G-note each with no sweat. When we arrived, Bumps led us to a table at the back where he greeted two guys, one black, the other Latino. The black cat's name was Claude, and the Latino's was Carlos. The Latino dude had bloodshot eyes that kept darting at us, and I figured he was strung out on some kind of drug, which made me nervous. I didn't like doing business with junkies; I'd seen too many of them rat on their friends for a fix.

Carlos reached into his pocket and handed Bumps a piece of paper.

Bumps put on his glasses and gazed at it for a few seconds. "You sure about this?"

"Bumps," the black dude cut in, "Carlos been driving for these here folks for years. If he say they trust him, then they gots to."

Bumps acknowledged that logic with a baleful look, folded the paper, and shoved it in his jacket.

It wasn't until we were in his big Caddie breezing along the freeway that he filled us in. He handed me the scrap of paper; it was a sketch of a road map. Carlos drove a truck for a big clothing warehouse near Lansing, and the next night he and another worker would be delivering thousands of dollars worth of men's and women's leather apparel to stores in the Grand Rapids area. The plan was for Top Cat and me to be at a truck stop on U.S. 96 when Carlos pulled in around ten o'clock. We'd highjack the truck, take it south with both Carlos and his helper inside, and drive to a side road south of Battle Creek where two guys would be waiting in a green Chrysler. They would hand us an envelope, we'd give them the keys to the truck, and we'd take the Chrysler. Carlos and his helper were to be tied up and blindfolded, and we'd drop them down a side road so they wouldn't be able to get to a phone, and then we'd take the envelope straight back to Bumps.

The heist went off exactly as planned, and TC and I made a thousand bucks each as promised, our biggest payday to date. It also sunk in later that we would have done major prison time if we'd been caught. My level of crime activity had elevated drastically.

CHAPTER 16

Tyrone and Buster

Shortly after the heist, a couple of Detroit Police officers came knocking at our apartment.

Tensions were high between blacks and Detroit police, plus TC and I worried that someone had ratted us out over the Bumps heist, so we instinctively went into a defensive mode. But they began asking questions not about us but about Tyrone, who shared the apartment with TC and me. When was the last time we saw him? What did he look like? What was he wearing? Did he have any relatives in the city? We didn't know what they had on Tyrone, but we clammed up. They kept asking whether he had any family in Detroit, and I finally told them his people lived in Plains, Georgia. At that point, they said we'd have to accompany them downtown.

As soon as they said that, TC and I sensed the worst. We didn't know what Tyrone had done, but somehow we knew it was going to come back on us. We were driven downtown

143

in the back of a police cruiser, and we never said much on the way. I had this unsettled feeling in the pit of my stomach. But we didn't go to police headquarters; instead, we pulled into the Detroit Receiving Hospital. My instincts told me that something was very wrong, but I had no idea what lay ahead.

The officers led us through a side entrance and onto a freight elevator, which took us down to the basement through a maze of dimly lit halls. It was apparent that the cops had made this trip many times before. Finally, we stopped in front of a large door.

"You know what this place is, son?" one of the cops asked.

On the door in bold black type was the word *Morgue.*

My heart began pounding. I nodded, and my throat went dry.

"There's a dead body inside here," he said softly. "We need one of you boys to identify it."

I prayed silently. "Oh, God, please don't let it be Tyrone!" Funny how quickly religion can be found when we're desperate.

I stood outside the door trembling. The officers showed some compassion, a rarity among Detroit cops back then. They allowed us a few minutes to prepare ourselves, and then they led us through the door into a large, dismal room that smelled strongly of antiseptic. A hospital attendant guided us to a row of steel gurneys. I could tell by the disinterested look on his face that he'd been a longtime employee of this morbid place.

As we approached the gurneys, I could make out the outlines of motionless bodies under the sheets. My heart was thudding like a bongo drum. The attendant glanced at the cop, waiting for the okay. The cop looked at Top Cat and me and then nodded. The man pulled back the sheet.

It *was* Tyrone!

His eyes were half open, and his skin was very pale. I'd seen corpses before and would again, but this was the first time I'd ever seen a murdered one. Death doesn't become anybody, but when it's somebody with whom you've been tight it's a sickening feeling. I stood in silence staring at his lifeless body for what seemed like a long time but was actually only about ten seconds.

"Is this here boy Tyrone Proctor?" the cop asked.

Choking back tears, I nodded yes.

He'd been stabbed to death. He'd left that evening around eight o'clock to hook up with a lady he'd met at a dance the night before. Witnesses had told police he'd been approached around ten o'clock by three guys, and an altercation had taken place. He'd been stabbed in the throat and chest and had died in hospital a few hours later.

For the next few days, Top Cat and I stayed locked up in the apartment and attempted to deal with the loss in our own ways. I kept thinking about Tyrone lying in the morgue, all alone, his eyes staring blankly into space. At times I wept openly, and in other moments anger and revenge overwhelmed me. I wanted retribution. Our gang swore vengeance, but nobody ever found out who the killers were. Tyrone became just another statistic in the Detroit City Morgue.

His death filled me with a ton of guilt, mostly because I'd known all along that he didn't have the warrior mentality that it took to be part of a gang. You've got to be either bad or treacherous to survive gang life, and he was neither. But he was always tagging along with us. I suppose he wanted to be part of something, to belong. Tyrone was just a big, strong country boy who'd been raised on a farm in Georgia. It was a place far removed from the dangerous streets of Motor City. Folks in Plains would leave their doors unlocked all the time and look after others like they were family. The dude was pure country and lacked street smarts, the kind of kid who never swore in front of girls. He used to chuckle at us when we gave him hell for not locking the apartment door or for wandering into hostile turf to visit with the girls.

I'd even warned him just a few days before his death that somebody was going to bust a cap in his ass if he kept messing with the girls of rival gang members. He hadn't taken the warning seriously.

A few days later, Tyrone was shipped back to Georgia for burial, dead at nineteen.

There is nothing glamorous about a player's life. I will never glorify the players' game. Nor is there any lasting security in it. But the truth is many times it was the players who fed me and put a roof over my head when I needed it most. It was the players who treated me with respect and gave me love when most of society shunned me. It was the players with whom I shared some of the best swinging times of my life. It was also the players who schooled me in the ways of the street: how to steal, rob, cheat, and lie. But I was growing tired of having to look over my shoulder all the time, tired of all the fighting and violence, tired of ducking the police, tired of my family being ashamed of me.

The most valuable advice I ever got about the streets

came one day from an old street hustler named Buster who had just got out of the hospital and was dying of cancer. Bumps decided to throw a party for him at the Chit Chat Lounge to lift his spirits. At one time, Buster had been among the most prominent players in the city, but when he went to jail for shooting a pimp the time inside finally cost him whatever he had, including his health.

During the party, he and I got to talking and laughing and having a good time, when suddenly he went all serious on me. "Look around this place, young blood," he said. "Whatcha see?" At first, I didn't know where he was coming from. Then he began to zero in on the older guys in the place. As he pointed to each of them, he shared some fascinating story of the dude's exploits. Sadly, each story ended with the guy's current situation. Not one of them had a fairy-tale ending. All these guys were just a heartbeat away from total disaster.

Buster was not just some pontificating fool; he was one of the most street-smart guys I ever knew, so when he talked I listened. The things he said about these guys blew my mind. Most of them looked like the homeless. He reflected on how each of them had been regarded as a prime-time player in his heyday. One guy had owned a big Caddie and once had six women hooking for him, yet there he was wearing shabby clothes and looking like death warmed over, munching Lifesavers to mask a terrible breath problem from rotted teeth. Another dude called Squeaky once drove a big Lincoln Continental and was reputed at one time to be the cleanest, best-dressed dude in all of Detroit. Poor guy now looked like a vagrant. I figured he was about sixty-five or seventy years old. Buster told me he wasn't yet fifty.

"That's what this kind of life do to you, boy," he said. "There ain't no security in the fraternity of players." He sighed, looking at me through bloodshot eyes. "We all talk a whole lot and pretend to be big-time, but ain't none of us got a pot to piss in!" Then he looked me straight in the eye. "Young blood, you smart, and you got lots of balls. So I'm gonna tell you this now: get out of this mess while the getting is still good. Get you a trade or some kind of skill, otherwise you gonna end up like all the rest of us: rotting in jail, living in dives, or being shot dead!"

Buster died a few months after our little talk. Poor dude was so broke Bumps had to pay for his funeral. At the wake, about fifty players and friends showed up and drank free booze, did some reefer, and spouted all kinds of affectionate things about him. Most of them, like Buster, lived on yesterday's memories and cheap wine. I sat, listened, and wondered who'd be paying for their plots after the Grim Reaper came for *them*. I thought of Buster that afternoon and grieved some. He died a poor man, but before they planted his soul he had planted some seeds of wisdom in mine. Sure, it took a few years before they blossomed, but eventually they took hold, and now I try to plant those seeds in the hearts of others.

I began to find myself observing the older players. As Buster had said, most of them lived in the projects and depended on government handouts. It was a depressing revelation and played heavily on my mind. It made me begin to seriously consider my future. I'd already begun to feel a strong sense that what I was doing was wrong. The values my parents had taught me were playing on my mind and forcing me to wrestle with my conscience. I began to question some things for the first time. For instance, why *were* so many of the oldtime players left with nothing? Hadn't they been making good money? Was I destined to end up like them? Would I even live to reach their age? Would my life end violently as Leroy's or Sonny's or Tyrone's had? How would I be able to cope with the streets and defend what was mine when I hit old age?

Reality was kicking in on me. I began to realize that all my skills and instincts had been geared for the street life, not the straight life. I sensed that my days on the street were numbered. Only a few years earlier, I had enjoyed the fights, but more and more the violence began to turn me off. I became more interested in dressing fancy and making out with the ladies. It seemed that every time I got into a fight I ruined some part of my wardrobe.

I really desired a change. Trouble was I didn't know where to begin. All I knew was that somehow I had to find a way out of the darkness.

CHAPTER 17

The Greatest

After the deaths of Sonny, Leroy, and Tyrone, I had enough of the violence of Detroit, and the winter of 1966 found me back in Toronto.

In early March, the buzz that Muhammad Ali was coming to Toronto to fight George Chuvalo electrified the city. Ali was at the height of his career, and "I am the greatest!" reverberated around the world from the most colourful self-promoter in sports history. Ali had just become heavyweight champion of the world with his upset victory over Sonny Liston in February of '64. He had defended once against Liston in May of '65 and also against former heavyweight champ Floyd Patterson in November of '65. This bout with Chuvalo was to be only his third title defence since winning the title. It was also Ali's first bout outside the United States, which was necessary because of his stand against the war in Viet Nam and the refusal of any American cities to host his fights. So it was getting a tremendous amount of front page media play around the world.

Then news came that he was not only coming to town but also was going to train at the Toronto Athletic Club, also known as Sully's after owner George "Sully" Sullivan — *my home gym!* Man, did I feel a jolt of excitement! I'd given up most of my thieving street ways, but hard times and I were still going steady, and I not only trained at Sully's but also worked there and lived there on the old sofa.

It was Sully who gave me my ring name — Spider — an identity that would stick with me for the rest of my life. Sully was watching me spar, and one day, as he tossed me a towel, he said, "You know, kid, you remind me a lot of Spider Webb." Elsworth "Spider" Webb was a highly ranked middleweight who fought out of Chicago at the time. He had fast hands, and he was tall and rangy like I was, and Sully said that I also had that quick, spiderlike quality the way I shot out my punches. Before Sully's comment, I just went by my own name, Charles, or Chuck, but I immediately took to the nickname. I thought it was cool, and Spider stuck.

Sully's house was a second home to me, and Sully was like a surrogate father. I went to his home many times. I was a kid of nineteen, and Sully and his wife fed me, cared for me, and guided me. There were many nights I'd leave Sully's home after dinner and head back to the sofa at the gym. I'd hang around the place on Saturdays and Sundays, work out, and then watch the fights and hockey games on the TV in the corner. I'd spend many hours after sparring sessions just sitting around in the company of the regulars at Sully's — a collection of colourful characters right out of a Damon Runyon column.

Sully's had the atmosphere of one of those great oldtime

boxing gyms that made you feel like you were caught in a time warp. It reeked of sweat and lingering cigar smoke, and the bare overhead bulbs gave the place a bright, warm feeling. In the middle of the gym was a twenty-foot ring with a bloodstained canvas, and beside it hung four tired-looking heavy bags and two speed bags. In the back were a musty dressing room and a shower. But there was something noble and appealing about Sully's; it had character, which most gyms today lack with their slick floors and bright fluorescent lights. And it was my home, the place where I spent the majority of my time, where I lived and trained and *mostly* left behind my old street ways.

My bed was the old leather sofa at the front of the gym, just below dingy, dusty old windows. In return for lodging, Sully expected me to keep the joint clean, which included sweeping the floors, cleaning the toilet and shower, and emptying the spit buckets.

When I got hungry or needed groceries, I'd slip back into my old habits and do some shoplifting in the storerooms of local restaurants. They were easy game. I'd case places where the washrooms were in the basements, because that was also where most storerooms would be. I'd go in carrying my boxing bag and order a coffee. Then I'd go downstairs to the bathroom. I always carried a screwdriver, and most storeroom locks were usually flimsy and easy to break: I copped canned fruit, steaks, pork chops, chicken, veal. I may have been broke, but I ate like the upper crust.

The day Ali arrived in town, I left the gym around eleven o'clock to do some road work. When I arrived back, both sides of the street were jammed with cars, and a huge crowd was hanging around the front door trying to get in. I had to shoulder my way up the flight of steps to the second floor. Then, when I went to enter, I came face to face with a heavy-set dude who put his hand on my chest.

"Ali's training," he growled, "it's two dollars to get in and watch." He was fronting me like I was a chump.

I shoved his hand away and was just about to get in his face when Sully hollered, "Hey, that's Spider. Let him through."

I pushed into the room, which was so packed it was hard to move, and I pressed my way toward the dressing room till I got to a roped-off area that separated the spectators from the media and VIPs. Some of the Toronto Maple Leafs were inside the VIP area: Eddie Shack, Dickie Duff, several others. Again I was waved through, and I felt pretty important stepping over that rope and joining those people, being in territory where you weren't allowed unless you were privileged.

In the dressing room, Muhammad was changing, and Black Muslim security guys were guarding the door. Then Jimmy Ellis came out of the room. Jimmy, of course, had grown up in Louisville with Muhammad and become one of his closest friends. Jimmy was a warm guy, a very spiritual Christian. We were introduced, and he gave me a warm smile. I went on to get to know Jimmy well. I met him many times afterward, and even sparred with him on occasion. We talked for about ten minutes, and I said, "Hey, Jimmy, I'd really love to meet the champ when he comes out." Jimmy said he'd set it up.

Then Angelo Dundee came out, one of the great icons of the fight game. Jimmy introduced us. Angie had that thick New York accent: "'Ey, nice to meecha, Spida. Howerya doin'?" He was very friendly and down to earth, as most fight people are. I started laying all this boxing history on him; all my life I'd been a fight fan, and I really knew my stuff. We talked about some of the people he had worked with, and he was surprised that I knew he'd trained Luis Rodriguez, a former world welterweight champion out of Puerto Rico. We also talked about another of his great welterweights, Carmen Basilio. Angelo was impressed that I knew so much about the fight game and about him. He realized that I was a knowledgeable fight guy, not just a spectator, and he assured me that I could meet Ali when he came out.

Finally, the door opened again, and Ali stepped into the room.

Man! Was I knocked out!

He had on a pair of red sweat pants and white laced-up ring shoes. *Nobody* wore *white* boxing shoes in those days! We were all still wearing the traditional, black ones. We knew that Ali was fast, but those white shoes made him even *look* fast, like some sort of god of speed.

People went nuts. About seven hundred had paid two dollars each to cram into the small gym, and they were all screaming "Ali-iii! Ali-iii!" The women were going bananas; they had never seen a guy like this. I had never seen a dude like him either. We're talking Elvis Presley worship. Michael Jackson worship. Beatlemania. It was like watching history unfold.

Everybody around him called him Champ, as they usually do with top fighters. In the midst of all the racket, Angelo yelled, "Hey, Champ, c'mere. I want ya to meet someone. I want ya to meet Spider."

As Ali approached, Jimmy Ellis piped up and said, "Hey, Champ, Spider says he can whip you!"

Ali turned on me. "You say that, nigger?"

I was looking into the face of the most famous human being on the planet, someone I had admired for years, and he had called me "nigger"! He also looked *huge*. He was tall at six foot three, but he was always on his toes, which made him seem another three inches taller. And he had filled out from his early days and now had large, muscular shoulders. Plus his *presence* made him seem even bigger. He seemed to loom over me, to look down on me. I felt tiny, and I'm six foot one.

And what a good-looking guy he was in the flesh! After his size, that was what struck me. I remember thinking, "Jesus, will you look at this guy? There's not a mark on his face!" At that time, he'd been heavyweight champion of the world for more than two years, but he'd still never been cut in a fight. And he had such beautiful features. Not feminine but classic. The straight nose, the high cheekbones, the thick eyebrows — handsome as hell!

Later, when I got to know him, I realized that he often used the *n* word just to shake people up and have some fun with them. But even then, in that moment, I saw the twinkle of mischief in his eye and the little smile on his lips, and I knew he wasn't saying it to be hurtful. He was saying it to be *playful*. I was amused and flattered that he would joke with me. I had no choice but to fall under his spell. So I played along.

I said, "Yeah, it's true, Champ, and if I gotta do it right here in front of all these people, then I'm gonna do it!" And I ripped off my jacket.

Ali ran back yelling, "No, Angie, help me. Jimmy, help me. He's comin' for me!"

Right away I felt a powerful affection for this guy. To be in the presence of Ali, to feel the love emanating from him, was one of the most moving experiences of my life. In a way, I think I know how Jesus' disciples felt in his presence. There was a sense of greatness, destiny, and mystical love that radiated from Ali that was so real you could *feel* it.

After a few moments of clowning, he shook my hand and said, "Hey, man, what's your name?"

I said, "Man, I'm Spider Jones."

Muhammad always had a heartfelt love for black people, his people, and it made me feel great.

I then said, "Champ, I know you gotta work out, can I get a quick picture with you?"

He agreed, and one of the gym regulars stepped forward and snapped a couple of quick pictures of us. Later I didn't know whether to laugh or cry when I saw the photos, because they were every amateur photographer's worst nightmare. One was a shot of the ceiling, and the other showed me standing beside somebody with no head from the nose up. I'd show people the photo, and they'd say, "Aw, man, you jivin' me. That ain't Ali." I'd say, "Yes, it is, man, that's Ali!" I got more pictures later, which proved it, but for a while no one believed me.

After our on-the-spot photo session, Ali climbed into the ring, and everyone was hypnotized by his moves. He did three fast rounds of shadow boxing — no gloves, just throwing out jabs and crosses, limbering up, and dancing around. He started out slowly, but even then you could see the blinding hand speed, and, as he warmed up, he started to move sooo fast. Unbelievable. The way he moved around the ring was like a huge cat, a panther. I'd never seen anything like it, and I'd seen a lot of boxers. Back and forth, back and forth, moving around the ring, along the ropes, his feet moving almost as fast as his hands. Throwing jabs, then rights, then flurries of seven or eight punches. It was a beautiful sight!

I watched Angelo, who was leaning forward, one foot on the ropes, chewing a wad of gum, watching Ali closely and talking to him all the time: "'At a boy, Champ, now back the other way. Now double up. Three-, four-, five-punch combination. Left hook, right hand. Left jab, right hand, left hook. Over the top. Underneath."

I was becoming more enamoured of Ali by the minute. He was doing something to me. He was changing me. First, he was changing the way I approached boxing. Before that day, I was a stand-up-straight boxer. I didn't have the flashy footwork, the smooth moves, but I knew I had the foot speed and the hand speed, so I started to emulate him. Many fighters did, but it wasn't good for our careers, because very few of us had his timing and what he called his "built-in radar system." He said he could "see" punches, see them shaping up, and he could slide away from them. Also, when other fighters tried to emulate his habit of dropping his hands to his waist, it led to more than a few unexpected knockouts.

On his third day in town, Ali was sparring with Tray Travis, a heavyweight who trained out of Sully's. The gym was packed with onlookers as usual, and I was over in the corner with some of the regulars working the heavy bag and keeping one eye on the action in the ring. It was a pretty one-sided sparring session. Travis was big and strong, but he was no match for Ali's speed. He may have been outclassed but it was the highlight of his life.

Travis left the ring for the showers, and Ali went to his corner to towel off, but he was hardly sweating. Angelo was talking to him, then all of a sudden Angie turned and looked around the gym. He called out, "Hey, kid, you want to work a couple of rounds? Move around with the Champ?"

Angie called all young fighters "kid," and five or six of us looked up. I wasn't sure which one of us he'd meant. I thought maybe he was joking. I looked around at the other guys and realized that I was the only guy that Angie and Muhammad knew pretty well and that he was talking to *me*. Angie wanted to get some more out of Muhammad that day.

In that moment, I had two thoughts. The first was "Wow! In the ring with Muhammad Ali!" I'd never dreamed of that. Then, as that thought sunk in, my second thought was "Man, you're not going to look good working out with the Champ in front of all these people." Plus don't think that it didn't occur to me, with our weight difference, that I could not only look bad but also get *hurt* bad! I was only a middleweight amateur, nineteen years old, and about 175 pounds. At 218 professional pounds, Ali could inflict damage on a guy my size that was scary.

I had to think fast, but it was the chance of a lifetime, and I figured that a workout between Muhammad and me would be mostly for movement and timing on his part. Heavyweights will sometimes spar with lighter-weight boxers to work on their timing because a lot of the big guys lack speed. Also, I knew that Ali had a reputation for not being especially hard on sparring partners, unlike some other top heavyweights, who enjoyed inflicting major damage in sparring sessions. For instance, I would never, under any conditions, have entered the ring to spar with Joe Frazier.

Joe was tough even on guys *bigger* than he was. He'd knocked out more than a few in training camps. I'd also seen George Chuvalo do enough damage to sparring partners to think that sparring with *any* heavyweight wouldn't be fun.

Nonetheless, I decided to go for it. Even if I got a bad ass whipping, I'd never get another chance like this. I called out, "Sure, Angie, but do you think the Champ can keep up to my speed?" When everyone laughed except Muhammad, I knew I was in for it.

I climbed into the ring with so many butterflies that I had a nauseous feeling in the pit of my stomach, like back when I first started on the smoker circuit. But this was a different kind of nervousness. Aside from the threat of getting hurt, it was the most overwhelming moment of my life. Fortunately for my health and our friendship, Muhammad was compassionate.

As far as hitting *him* went, I didn't even try at first. I was too much in awe. That happens a lot when you see an amateur and a pro in the ring. The amateur has so much respect for the pro and knows what the pro can do — that he is capable of really busting you up if you go all out on him. But I loved this guy. The last thing I was going to do was be stupid enough to go all out. A guy like me could get lucky and land a shot that could do some fluke damage that could jeopardize his upcoming fight.

Ali started moving around me, playing with me, throwing out jabs that were blurs. I'd seen as a spectator what he did with other sparring partners; now I was in the ring and seeing it up close. I could only think, "Wow! This is as fast as I've ever seen any human being move." His gloves were red streaks shooting past my nose. And he timed his shots so that they barely touched me. He would snap out a left and only lightly tap my headgear. His hands were so quick I couldn't see them coming. I couldn't mount any kind of defence against such speed. The jab would come and go before I could react. It made me just shake my head in admiration: "Wow!"

Halfway through the first round, I loosened up, and my nerves settled down. Ali could tell that I was feeling better. He said, "C'mon, man, hit me." So I tried to slip in punches, the odd dig to the body, and he let me. I even hit him a few good left jabs because he let me. I hit him with a couple more jabs, and he came right back with a right hand — bam! He wanted to make a workout of it, not just waste his time. So he let me land a few more without once landing a solid one back on me.

I was considered a fast fighter with a good pair of hands, and Muhammad got to trash-talking me. "I'm gonna whup your sorry ass, chump. You know you got no chance." He rolled his right hand around five or six times like a windmill, almost hypnotized me, and then he snuck out a left jab and shot it at me and said, "It's all over, baby." Then he danced away and started yelling at the press, "Get a picture of this, boys — I'm gonna knock Spider on his butt." And I thought he'd do it, because he closed in and laid a combination on me: boom-boom-boom, like lightning. But he didn't land any solid shots, and he never tried to hurt me.

We went a couple of rounds that day, and my stock around the gym shot through the roof. I'd been welcomed into that exclusive circle of boxers who could rightly say they'd sparred with Ali. Pretty rarefied company, and I felt great. I could honestly say that I got my ass kicked by the greatest.

Ali-Chuvalo I – 1966

I hung out with Muhammad Ali and his entourage quite a bit over the two weeks leading up to the first Chuvalo fight in Toronto. Often, in the mornings, we'd go to the restaurant in the Seaway Towers Hotel, where they were staying. The first thing Ali would do was head to the kitchen and look for Nick, the little Greek cook. Muhammad had got it into his head that he didn't want anybody but Nick cooking breakfast for him. He'd call for Nick, and, when Nick showed up, he'd dance around him, jabbing and shadow-boxing him. Nick was about five foot five, almost a full foot shorter than Ali, and they sure made a strange sight dancing around the kitchen, chasing each other, Nick trash-talking Ali in a thick Greek accent. It was incongruous as hell, but people loved it. Even having breakfast with Ali was an event.

Several times I went jogging with Ali and Jimmy along the lakefront across the road from their hotel. One time I even caught a nap on Ali's bed after a hard jog.

In the evenings, we'd go to the movies or a restaurant or take long walks, and when you hung with Muhammad you hung with the whole entourage: Angie, Jimmy, his personal photographer Howard Bingham, the Black Muslim security guys, his rub-down guy, plus whichever sparring partners he had come in. They went everywhere together!

In those days, I seldom had money on me, but when I was with Ali I didn't need any; his entourage paid for everything — meals, movies, everything. One night I got a phone call from Angelo, who asked me if I was up to showing them downtown. Was I! I was thrilled! They picked me up at Sully's, and I slid into the back of the stretch limo with Ali, Jimmy, and Angelo. Up front were Ali's manager, Herbert Muhammad, Howard Bingham, and Sam Saxon of Black Muslim security, whom they called Captain Sam.

Right off the bat, Ali started hollering, "Spider Jones . . . Spider Jones . . . he's so bad he can't be had! He's a baaaaad dude!" Then he reached out and jabbed at me and began to bellow out "Stand by Me," the song he'd recorded a few years before. I jumped in, and we jammed all the way downtown. It was super cool to be in the company of these guys. They were all straight-up and friendly. You could sense a strong bond of affection between them. I was flattered to be accepted as part of their crew.

We went to Yonge Street, Toronto's main drag, and it didn't take long before there were people all around us. One skinny white kid about half Ali's size was pressing in, trying to get an autograph, when Ali said to him, "Hey, come here, boy."

The kid came forward, and Ali turned to me and said, "Spider, do you recognize this guy?"

I said, "Naw, I don't know him, Champ."

Then Ali said, "I know who you are, man."

The kid said, "Yeah?" He was a little excited that somebody like Ali knew him.

And Ali said, "Yeah, you the white boy that called me nigger. I'm gonna whip your butt."

It was March and still pretty cool in Toronto, and Ali had on a half-length leather coat, which he tore off, and the kid, for some reason, could read Ali, knew he was just joking, so he tore off his coat and came after Ali too. By then, with all the commotion, traffic was stopped for two blocks in both directions. People had actually gotten out of their cars and rushed to the area. They were also running out of the stores calling out, "Hey, Champ!" And there he was dancing around the street with this kid, playing with him, slapping out at him, and saying, "Oh, what a feeling it must be to be hit by a man you can't see!" At one point, he ran back from him and put his hands up to cover himself and said, "Man, don't hurt me. Help me, Spider." When the skit finally wound down, he signed autographs, let people take pictures, and talked to everyone.

I admired Ali for being so full of life and always so giving of himself, but I also admired his serious side and his convictions. Away from all the people and the fanfare, there were times when he'd get really quiet. You'd see him lost in thought, introspective, often thinking about his people, black people. That's the part of him I got to see that a lot of people didn't. Sometimes you'd wonder what was wrong. Then he'd sit down and talk about things on his mind. Muhammad would talk, and everybody would listen.

We knew he was fighting the U.S. military because he

didn't believe in the Vietnam War, but that didn't seem to embitter him. He'd talk about it sometimes, about his upcoming exile. He was having a tough time getting fights. Even in Toronto he was hounded. Conn Smythe, the former Canadian army colonel who owned Maple Leaf Gardens, where the fight was set, called Muhammad a "traitor" and even tried to stop the fight from taking place there.

Other times we'd sit around and talk about race relations, and I realized that, for all the hatred directed at him at the time, he wasn't capable of hatred himself. I remember Angelo saying, "I don't think Mo has it in him to hate *anybody*." I found it kind of funny that Angelo and a few of the others would call Ali "Mo." Of course, his name was *Mu*hammad, not *Mo*hammed. But Ali always just let it pass.

And he was a contradiction when it came to women. That spring I saw literally hundreds of women throw themselves at him, and he flirted with so many who crossed his path, but I never actually saw him with a woman. I believe that the strict Muslim code about extramarital relations had already taken hold of Muhammad and that he'd changed his ways with women from his early days. He'd say all kinds of beautiful things to girls (even in a crowd he'd flirt), and they'd offer themselves up, but he didn't try to pick them up. When he was in Toronto, he was married to Sonja Roy, and she was breathtaking — beautiful light caramel straight hair, eyes that could melt you. But she wasn't with him while he was in town, and he just hung with the guys.

Also, Muhammad never drank and never swore. He didn't allow booze around him, and he didn't like people swearing around him. He'd tell you in a second, "Don't swear, man!" He had those strong Muslim beliefs, but there were times

167

THE SPIDER JONES STORY

when they got on his nerves, because he was a free spirit. The Muslim brothers were close to him at all times, mostly the Muslim security guys, called the Fruit of Islam. They stayed mostly in the background, but they were always around him, making their presence known, and Ali would get mad if they didn't leave him some space. Don't think he didn't turn around sometimes and snap at these guys, "Back off, man." One time he lost his temper, slammed the door, and said, "Man, can't you cats just *lighten up!*"

On the day before the bout, Muhammad took the money they'd collected at the door at Sully's and donated it to the gym, several thousand dollars in all. Sully couldn't believe it. That money soon turned into much-needed new bags and equipment.

Also that day, Ali was dancing around in the ring when there was a commotion in a corner of the gym. Everyone looked around, and coming through the crowd was none other than big Jim Brown, followed by Howard Cosell. Jim was long retired from the Cleveland Browns and was already a movie star by then. They'd come in to do the TV colour commentary of the fight for the network. And right behind them was Joe Louis. George Chuvalo's manager, Irving Ungerman, had actually brought Joe to town as a boost to the Chuvalo camp, and I was flattered that Joe remembered me from my days at the Big D as a kid.

The media pressed around Jim, and it became a wild press scrum — flashes popping, reporters shoving for position and yelling out questions. Jim was wearing an expensive, dark sharkskin suit cut to fit tightly, and, with his back to me, all I could see was the suit stretched across those massive shoulders of his. I knew that Jim was a big guy, but I was surprised to see that he was *way* bigger in the chest and arms than Ali.

When it was my turn to meet him, he stuck his huge hand out, looked me right in the eye, and said, "How are ya doin', my man?"

I thought I was bad, but, man, when he looked at me I knew what bad really was. I knew I was looking into the face of one of the baddest cats I'd ever seen. You could see something intense in his eyes. I realized then why he'd been so unstoppable as a running back, why opposing players had given him so much room, why they'd *feared* going near this man.

Ali wrapped it up in the ring, regaining his position as the centre of attention. His group decided to go downtown for dinner.

Angelo turned to me and said, "Spider, where's a good place?"

I suggested the Colonial Tavern, a large, classy, downtown meeting place.

Ali showered and changed, and he and his whole entourage, plus Brown and Cosell, headed downtown. The Colonial had huge round booths that could seat maybe a dozen people, so we got one, and Ali held court while the whole restaurant was focused on our table.

Cosell had a reputation for being pompous and opinionated, but I liked Howard because he always told it like it was. Actually, he would have a profound influence on my radio career. Many people today say that I'm one of the few people on radio who tell it like it is. Well, I got that approach from Howard. He didn't mince words. If he had something to say, he said it, and I respected him for that. However, a radio career for me was still several lifetimes away and not even on my mind in those days.

Dinner with Ali and Jim was one of the most entertaining times of my life. Ali kept getting on Jimmy, getting him going. Jim would just be sitting there maybe talking to me or someone else, and Ali would pipe up: "Jimmy, you ain't bad. You sitting up here looking like you bad, but you ain't bad. *I'm* bad! I'm gonna whip you here and now!"

Jimmy would look at him and just roll his eyes. He'd say, "Man, you a damn fool if you think you can whup me. I'd get my hands on you, and I'd crush you."

Ali would shoot back, "Jimmy, you can't whip me, what you talking like that for? You ain't bad."

They went back and forth like that all night, but you could see that there was a real respect between them, and we all cracked up when they got going.

After dinner was done, out on Yonge Street, Ali got to dancing around Jim, throwing jabs, and carrying on jiving him.

Jim said, "You better get out of my face, nigger."

And then they got into it back and forth on the sidewalk, stopping traffic and drawing another crowd.

Ali wailed at the top of his lungs, "Jim Brown, you the *second* baddest cat on Earth. I'm number one baddest!"

It was great fun, and I remember thinking that Ali might be able to cut Jim to ribbons with his hands, but if Jim ever got the bear hug on him for serious he'd be Ali no more.

Ali had George Chuvalo on his mind a lot just before the fight.

George came to fight every time, with no nights off, and

Ali knew it. He'd heard about George, and he was concerned. Ever since he'd hit town, he'd heard guys talking about George. Not the guys in the media — those duds don't know a left hook from a fishhook; no, Ali kept hearing rumblings about George from guys in the gyms, from guys who knew the real score: sparring partners, trainers, ring rats.

George trained out of the Lansdowne Gym in those days, but occasionally he stopped by Sully's, and we just sort of continued our friendship from our days at the Big D. Sometimes I'd head up to the Lansdowne to see George, and I'd shoot the breeze with Teddy McWhorters, jiving about the good times in Detroit. Teddy was an old Alabama boy — he'd come north with Joe Louis in the 1930s — and he had a lot of colourful stories about those early days with Joe.

In those days, I'd also become close with George's family, in particular his third son, Georgie Lee. Of the four boys, Georgie was probably the most like his dad in looks and build and for having an interest in boxing, and I started to train him at Sully's when he was only five years old. He was like a kid brother to me.

But there was no question that Muhammad was concerned about George. He brought it up with me several times. He knew George and I were good friends. One time Ali came right out and said to me, "Man, that cat's never been down. I been down twice, and I'm the champion of the world. I'm the greatest. How come this cat's never been down?" It was bothering him.

It put me in a spot because I didn't want to betray George, so all I could say was "You know what, Muhammad, he's a tough dude. The baddest cat I ever saw." I found myself torn. It was upsetting because I had so much affection and respect for both of these guys, and I didn't want to say anything out of line.

I recall listening to Ali and his handlers talk about George: "Watch him, Ali, or he'll turn this into a telephone booth brawl," boxing lingo for a nasty fight fought at very close quarters. "He'll hit you on the breaks. He'll step on your toes. He'll do *anything* it takes to win." I listened, and I knew that all these reports were completely true — George was merciless in the ring.

I thought, before the fight, that it probably would go all the way and that Ali would likely win on a decision. I didn't think Ali had the kind of power it would take to knock George out, and I didn't think George would be able to catch Ali to knock him out, because Ali was just too fast and too skilful at slipping punches.

Finally, fight night arrived.

I walked into Maple Leaf Gardens as part of Muhammad Ali's camp carrying a gym bag. I was right behind Jimmy Ellis and Angelo Dundee. For an unemployed nineteen year old, this was heaven. I looked around, and people were pleading for tickets, and scalpers were getting big bucks, but there I was walking straight in with Ali's crew. I was one of the boys. Man, I felt great that night! I was right at ringside in Ali's corner the whole night.

Ali's plan was to run and dance away from George, to dance away all night, and he tried, but fifteen rounds is a long time to dance, and when he realized that wasn't going to work he mixed in. They traded a lot of blows, and George hit him everywhere — from the kneecaps to the ribs. George wore Muhammad down with heavy, thumping body shots, and they put wariness in Ali's head. Ali claimed that Chuvalo had hit him below the belt on a few occasions, but the fact was it was almost impossible to catch Ali with a solid head shot. George tried, but Ali always pulled away. George fought like a warrior, and Ali came out of that fight slowed up. He urinated blood for days after the bout.

After the fight, some people tried to say that it never was an official title fight, merely a "heavyweight showdown," but history recorded it as a fifteen-round unanimous decision for Muhammad in defence of his world title.

Muhammad and George would go on to fight a similar brawl in Vancouver in 1972 — that one a twelve rounder — that would also go the distance with Ali again winning on points, but it turned out that I'd called that first fight in Toronto right on all counts.

CHAPTER 19

The Most Feared Address in America

After the Ali-Chuvalo fight, I needed to get some money together, so I headed back to Detroit to line up some smokers. It would be my final crack at trying to make it work in Motor City, and this attempt would blow up in a way I couldn't have imagined.

At first, I stayed at my parents' crib in Windsor, but I didn't feel cool about going back to what I'd been trying to flee for years. I was now twenty years old, and to be back in that tiny sweatbox with eleven other bodies was too depressing.

Also, two weeks after I arrived, the police busted me on an old assault warrant, some chump charge about a guy I'd beaten up the year before for bad-mouthing one of my sisters. I served sixty days in the county jail.

A month after release, I was busted again. This time for shaking down a rival gang member for a lumpy-assed watch he'd probably stolen in the first place. So I shook another thirty days in the joint.

173

My macho punk attitude was painting a bull's eye on my ass and making me a lot of enemies. Among my worst were the Windsor cops, who'd declared war on me. I decided to slip across to Detroit and lay low at my sister's crib.

I also went back to hanging out on the streets and clubs. But I sensed something different this time. In previous years, the jive had been all about baseball players and boxers. Now the most heated verbal exchanges were targeted at the Detroit police. When these men got on the topic of the po-lice, it was with bitter condemnation. Back then the Detroit police had developed a deadly reputation for the brutal ways that they dealt with blacks. Some of the dudes who frequented the barbershop were admittedly hustlers, players, and gangsters, but the majority were ordinary, hard-working taxpayers, men who worked long days to pay the rent, put groceries on the table, and put clothes on their kids' backs — and their anger was building.

What made the situation even more volatile was the impunity with which the cops committed their brutish acts. They'd storm into our homes, after-hours joints, bars, clubs, community centres, and other black hangouts as if we had no rights. I had it happen to me on a couple of occasions. They'd bust down the door, stick a gun in my face, and whack me with the big nightstick, and I had to stand there, blood boiling, while they taunted me with racial slurs, questioned my manhood, and insulted my lady. I knew they were praying for me to break bad. If I had, it would have been game over!

One night the cops raided a crib while we had a card game going on. We weren't doing any harm, none of us had committed any crime . . . of late. We were just playing some cards, shooting a little craps, and chilling out. Suddenly, there's a loud banging on the door, and next thing we know the Man's in the house hollering all this "nigger" and "coon" crap and shoving us around. They claimed they'd got complaints about too much noise from other tenants in the building, and they forced us to strip down to our undergarments to see if we were packing weapons or drugs. We did as we were ordered.

So there we were standing around with nothing on but drawers. It was particularly embarrassing for one of the brothers named Amos. He was wearing a pair of the funkiest-looking dingy white shorts I'd ever seen. They had a skid mark running up the back so wide you could have played a street hockey game on it. In the front was a large yellow stain of dried piss. Amos was on Front Street, and everybody was peepin' his whole card. Man, it was tough not to bust a gut. Even the cops got to laughing. This one big, lard-assed cop with a thick southern drawl, who looked like he was straight off the Mississippi bayou, got to signifying on Amos.

"Boy," he laughed, "you about the stankiest lookin' nigger I ever done seen." He was cracking up.

Truth be told, Amos had always been hard on the nostrils. Seeing him there in his underwear was a hilarious spectacle: a tall, dark, crusty-looking brother with a pair of legs so skinny it looked like he had to tie knots in them to make knees. No doubt he'd been wearing those shorts for a month of Sundays. Man, he was a funky trip!

Even under those insulting conditions, it took all my composure to hold back from laughing. I even closed my eyes and tried to pretend I was somewhere else. It didn't work. I lost control and busted out. Big mistake!

The cop with the southern drawl came flying over and smacked me upside my head. The blow shook me up pretty good. Then he got up in my face with a mixture of profanities and racial slurs. It took all my willpower to stay cool. The worst thing about him was his breath. I stood there, my ears ringing from the blow, trying to hold back, and his breath was so bad my eyes watered. He jumped all over me, said I had an attitude problem. Warned me that one more sound and we were all going for a trip to Belle Isle. That cooled me out.

Belle Isle is a small island in the Detroit River just off the downtown shore. It was supposed to be a park, but it was about as lawless as Central Park after midnight. It was an unpatrolled area, and all kinds of attacks, gang fights, and atrocities went on out there. I knew a girl who'd been raped and murdered out there. I'd also heard too many stories about brothers taken there and getting badly busted up or not returning at all.

Even worse than a trip to Belle Isle was a trip "downtown," code for Detroit City Police Headquarters, 1300 Beaubien Street. For blacks, 1300 Beaubien was the most feared address in America, the place where, as one cop told us, "loud-mouthed niggers go to die!" In the basement of that place, many blacks were beaten. To Detroit blacks, it was like Gestapo or KGB headquarters.

Detroit police, when they did this, the whole time they were calling you every foul name they could think of; your daddy was every foul thing they could think of; your momma and sister were every foul thing they could think of. They spewed hate and spit right in your face. It was to rile you so you would squirm against the cuffs, to get you angry enough to resist. Not that you could have resisted. It just made it more fun for them. The purpose was to beat a confession out of you. They always got their confessions in the end. They'd tell you what to confess to. That went on for years in Detroit.

But the big, boag-ass cop was right about my attitude. I'd never liked being gangstered by anybody. He kept staring at me, and I eyed him back. It was a chump's play. He popped me upside the head again so hard my ears rang. "Strip down to ya' bare ass, boy!" he shouted. "Right now, boy, or we gonna beat yo' ass all night long!" It was his rules, his game. The last thing I wanted was one of those good old-fashioned Detroit police ass whippings. I got down to the skin in a hurry. Then the sadistic dude ordered everybody in the place to laugh at me. I was standing buck naked in front of my boys with my family jewels hanging there like Christmas tree ornaments. It was one humiliating experience. I took a lot of heat from my boys after that.

When the cops eventually left, they swung with our booze. Told us if they had to come back we'd find ourselves in the obituary column.

But winds of change were blowing up a new breeze that was going to blow Motor City to hell!

For one thing, the heat drove people crazy that year. Our houses and apartments were like ovens, which drove everyone into the streets. Ghetto folks get belligerent when it gets too hot. The heat steals your sleep, your sanity. Makes you short tempered. There was no escape. No air-conditioning, no swimming pool, no shade. Just waves of heat coming off the pavement, where folks killed time by getting drunk, getting high, and getting crazy. We'd be out there shucking, jiving, and chilling over a drink, and then suddenly somebody would break bad, and then came the beating, stabbing, or shooting.

One day we were hanging with some foxes at the corner of Grand River and Hudson, and one of the guys had brought along an acoustic guitar, so we were chirping out some tunes when an altercation broke out across the street. Two older black dudes were arguing over a bottle of cheap wine. They began throwing down on one another. And one of the dudes landed a big shot that sent the other one crashing to the pavement. Then some other dude jumped to his rescue with a straight razor and got to slicing like a butcher on his block. Others leaped into the fray, and before you knew it the thing escalated into an all-out brawl. It was blood, fists, boots, and razors. As sickening as it was, the sad fact was that such brawls were a regular thing.

Somebody hollered, "Look out! He got a gun!"

Then the sound of gunfire exploded. Pop! Pop! Pop, pop! Four or five times. Then somebody returned the fire. Pop! Pop! Pop!

Man, we hit the pavement and scrambled behind some parked cars, and the crowd ran in every direction. Then came the familiar sound of sirens in the background.

When the smoke cleared, a couple of bodies were sprawled in the middle of Hudson Street. Another one was lying on the sidewalk, groaning. The closest body to us lay motionless in a pool of blood. Man, I was shook up over the whole thing. It doesn't matter how much violence you see, it's still tough to witness. The next day we heard that one of the guys had died on the street. There had been three other

The city was going from bad to crazy. Cheap guns — so-called Saturday Night Specials — all of a sudden became easy to purchase in the 1960s, and they changed the rules of the street. There was no need to earn respect in the old-school ways anymore. Why waste time fighting when you could blow somebody away? You could look at some kid the wrong way, and he might smoke you. Murder came easy.

I was living at Rosemary's place, on San Juan, in a relatively nice, leafy suburb in the north end, away from the tenements, desperation, and concrete of downtown. Rows of well-kept houses and neat lawns. It was a neighbourhood where successful blacks moved once they'd made it, the lucky few who got jobs on the lines at the Big Three auto makers. As soon as they got that good hourly rate, they were gone from downtown and only came back on Friday and Saturday nights. Rose's husband, Charlie Garrett, was a solid guy with a good job on the line at Chrysler, and he was a union steward to boot. In the black world in the '60s, that was about as good as upward mobility got.

Marvin Gaye lived around the corner. Marvin was Detroit's Main Man in those days. He'd just had a big hit with "How Sweet It Is to Be Loved by You." When Charlie told me he knew Marvin, I figured he was jiving me. "Yeah, you know Marvin Gaye like I know the pope," I said. So Charlie took me around to Marvin's crib, and we partied and sang long into the night.

I hooked up with Marvin a couple of times after that. We would cruise around town and go to the fights. One time we hit Tiger Stadium to catch the Tigers and the Yankees.

Marvin enjoyed hanging with me because I knew a lot of fighters, and he loved talking about boxing. Then he moved to L.A., and we lost contact. He was a sweet guy. It was a crime how his habits destroyed his talent.

Although I enjoyed living with Rose, I spent most of my time downtown. I hooked up with a couple of small-time players, and we ran dice and card games. I also did a little bootlegging on the side with a dude called Lanky because of his skinny, six-foot-three frame. He and his daddy ran an illegal still in the basement of their house. They had a prosperous thing supplying east-side bootleggers with homemade corn liquor and peach wine. Lanky's old man cut Lanky, Top Cat, and me in for a piece of the action for peddling his booze at dances. Truthfully, I didn't understand how anybody could stomach that nasty-tasting poison. And you dared not light a match around Lanky's dad's basement-brewed corn liquor. It was two hundred proof, and, being almost pure alcohol, it could have blown your ass to the moon. I gave it a sip once. Have mercy! Once was enough!

I was still totally captivated by the fast-paced nightlife and party attitude of downtown Detroit. There was always somewhere to go, something to do. Nightclubs, roller rinks, boxing gyms, soul music, fancy clothes, sports, foxy ladies! No one who actually lived in Detroit ever called it Detroit. To downtowners, it was just *The Big D*. We always knew when people were from out of town, because they actually called the place Detroit. Some said De-*troy*-it, and some said De-*troyt*. Either way, to us they were rubes or hayseeds.

I also loved Detroit's soul cuisine; soul food was everywhere. So was the delicious scent of soul food when folks were barbecuing. We called it 'cue time! Come the weekend,

I was a guest on Don Cherry's popular TV show, *Grapevine*, in 1987.

Cito Gaston, Manager of the Toronto Blue Jays and winner of back-to-back World Series wins in '93 and '94, became a good friend.

For several years I worked at The Fan 590 in Toronto, Canada's number one sports radio station. Far right: my producer, George Stroumboulopoulos, who is now at MuchMusic.

Here I deliver an inspirational message to a group of high school students in the Toronto area in 2002.

Baseball Hall of Famer and Cy Young Award winner, Fergie Jenkins, is an old childhood pal.

With my wife Jackie and good friend Muhammad Ali.

I toured in 1991 with Charlie Hodge, left, and Gary Wayne Bridges and their Elvis Tribute Revue. Hodge was one of Elvis' best friends.

With former Middleweight Champion, Jake LaMotta, The Raging Bull.

Floyd Patterson was the first man ever to re-capture the World Heavyweight title.

I've known heavyweight champion Lennox Lewis since he was fourteen years old.

This is one of my R&B groups, Spider Jones and The Fabulous Web, in 1969.

My family (clockwise from top): James, Charlie, Shelley, Jackie and Jennifer.

A promo shot from the movie I made with Tony Curtis,
Title Contender.

Hosting my radio show on CFRB in Toronto, Canada's number one AM station.

I graduated from Seneca College in Radio and Broadcast Journalism with honours and made the Dean's List in 1982.

Dianne Cunningham, Minister of the Ontario Ministry of Colleges and Universities, presented me with the Premier's Award for Outstanding Achievement in the Arts in 2001.

With colourful Toronto Maple Leaf tough guys, Tie Domi and
Darcy Tucker.

With "The Greatest of All Times," Muhammad Ali.

Don King, the self-proclaimed King of Boxing Promoters, gave me an award in 1986 for my pro boxing reports.

A promo shot clowning with George Chuvalo from the TV series, *Famous Knockouts.*

Working a fight for TSN with sports columnist Stephen Brunt and Lennox Lewis, then World Heavyweight Champion.

Michael Landsberg of TSN's hit sports talk show, *Off the Record*, is cruisin' for a bruisin'!

everybody got the barbecue going, and the sweet sound of soul music rocked the air.

But we could tell as spring turned to summer that something different was also in the air. Something bad was coming.

CHAPTER 20

Murder City Burns

Too many storm clouds of racial unrest had been gathering over the city for too long. The murder rate skyrocketed to over seven hundred that year, a U.S. per capita record. Motor City became Murder City, U.S.A. A sickening title, especially since buried in that notorious claim was the fact that it was black on black crime, much of it among our youth.

Blackbottom was primed to blow. Like the calm before a terrible storm, there was an odd, edgy tranquillity to the city in the early evening hours of Saturday, July 23, 1967, but the anger on the street was so palpable you could *feel* it like heat from a fire pit. Also, the temperatures had been in the high nineties for weeks, setting records and straining everyone's nerves to the breaking point.

That evening began quietly enough. I was with Rosemary and Charlie. We were cruising down 12th Street in Charlie's sleek new '66 Chrysler New Yorker, one of those big showboat cars of the 1960s with the massive chrome bumpers and grille and just as massive dashboards with all the fancy knobs and dials. Also with us were my older sis, Barbara, and TC. The radio was tuned to Detroit's top soul station, WCHB.

We were headed, as we always did on Saturday nights, to the maze of black-owned and -operated shops, restaurants, and nightclubs downtown. Blackbottom had a kind of funky, bluesy, Harlem-west feel to it, and it was the place to go on weekends. After the bars closed, we headed uptown to an after-hours joint in the north end. These clubs were known as blind pigs and sold bootlegged booze and beer as well as drugs under the table after everywhere else had closed down. The cat who ran the place was our old rounder and gambler friend Sampson.

We left around 2:30 a.m. to head back downtown, to another blind pig, when Barb noticed a red glow in the night sky, from downtown. "Something's burning up!" she commented.

Something sure as hell was. I'd never seen so much smoke.

There had been major rioting in Watts, in L.A., and in Harlem two summers before, and then just a few weeks earlier there had been bad rioting in Newark, New Jersey. When, we'd wondered, was Detroit in for it?

We figured it was a big building on fire. As we drew closer, we could hear the wail of fire sirens, and then a dozen police cruisers screamed past us. We turned onto 12th Street and headed toward Clairmount, but we could only drive a block because the police had 12th Street barricaded. We parked and walked to the blind pig, figuring we'd have a look at the source of the smoke later.

Generally, the pig we entered was a raucous after-hours hot spot, but on this night the mood was anything but festive. It was sullen and ugly. Stories were circulating about how the cops had thrown down a couple of young brothers the night before. The attack had come from the "Big Four," a term of derision that black folks had pinned on Detroit's much-feared and ludicrously named Morality Squad.

There wasn't much "moral" about those dudes. They used their badges as an excuse to beat on blacks at will. This latest was just another of the endless attacks and cold-blooded brutality they served up on Detroit's black kids. Stories of atrocities at the hands of rogue white cops had been circulating for so long you almost became deadened to them. Stories would surface, people would mutter, the stories would fade, and the anger would diffuse.

But this night something was different. That night people were *listening*, the mutters were threats of vengeance, and the anger wasn't diffusing — it was spreading.

The night before, the Big Four pulled the black kids over simply because they were cruising the downtown in a big, shiny Cadillac. The cops had no idea the car belonged to the kids' father, a successful dentist: to them, any brother driving an expensive machine was a pimp, a gangster, or a drug dealer. The two kids were handcuffed, hauled away, and beaten bloody. One kid ended up with a broken jaw and the other with other multiple injuries. One of the cops shoved the barrel of a gun so far down the kid's throat he puked.

A Detroit black parent's worst fear was of a son getting pulled over by the police, especially at night. Parents knew their sons were going to be brutalized, and many a mother said a prayer when her son walked out the door.

Another story circulating that night had Detroit police busting into the Algiers Motel two days earlier and shooting and killing three black kids whom they believed were gang members. But they were the wrong kids.

Both stories had hit the papers and proved to be true, but of course the newspaper accounts were sketchy and sanitized, and the dirty details only went out on the black grapevine. So Detroit was festering.

"I'm tired of those honky pigs messing with us!" a voice boomed.

We looked around. It was the voice of a big, mean-looking dude wearing a doo-rag, a cheap wig. I realized he was Rico Carter, one of 12th Street's most dangerous bangers. Rico was one of those natural-born street soldiers who'd grown up in the Brewster Projects and who always seemed to be looking to kick it or stick it with somebody. An evil guy who would put a knife in your ribs or a cap in your ass without a thought. How many had he already killed in his young life? He was full of anger and hatred, and that night he wanted trouble.

"I'm sick of seeing the home boys beaten on!"

"I hear you, brother," another angry voice answered from across the room.

Someone else said that the police had just raided another after-hours club and that eighty people had been taken down hard. Again the cops had been vicious, just to make a point. But that night a mob of young blacks gathered outside the joint had pushed back. The cops had called for backup, the brothers had called in friends, a street brawl had exploded, and trouble had rippled out like waves in a filthy pond.

Police had been raiding blind pigs for years. Blacks went to them because we weren't welcomed anywhere else, and *still* the Man came and got us.

As the mood in the room heated up, I began to get a cold chill. Not that the brothers didn't have plenty to be angry about, but I sensed that major trouble was brewing. "Let's split," I said, and we headed for the door.

Just as we were walking out of the door of the club, a bottle crashed against the brickwork beside us, and shards of sharp glass sprayed back at us. Rose screamed and put up her arm to cover her face.

Then about a block up the street an explosion blew out a storefront's plate-glass window and sprayed it into the street in front of us. Incredibly, as flames and acrid black smoke filled the street — and our nostrils — people dodged the fire to run inside to grab goods.

Rosemary gripped Charlie's arm and said, "Lord, what's happening?"

I realized then that the city was going.

We had to get out of there, but first we had to make it to the car.

Then everything happened at once. The riot took on a life of its own so quickly we were caught, as in a grass fire fanned by the wind. It surrounded us. Down the block, people were running through the smashed-down front door of another store, a grocery store. Next door to it, people were walking through the gaping, blown-out front of a variety store and walking back out with baskets filled with merchandise, picking their way through the glass and debris covering the floor and sidewalk. Another Molotov cocktail went through another plate-glass window — more debris was blown into the street. A brick went through another window. A chair through another. More fires were sprouting. Mattresses, doors off buildings, furniture, all were being thrown into the street, soaked in gasoline, and lit in huge bonfires. People were running in every direction. The crash of glass was everywhere.

This was the heart, soul, and centre of black Detroit, going up in flames. It was like some sort of spontaneous social combustion, with fires flaring up in all directions all at once. More sirens, and now, here and there, the sporadic pop-pop-pop of gunfire, and we knew people were dying.

A man raced past us with a portable TV set under his arm. Another was trying to balance a stack of hats, the expensive, wide-brimmed white Panamas favoured by young dudes in that part of town. He looked almost comical wobbling bowlegged down the street. All around us silhouettes and dark figures were moving, running, throwing, dancing like crazed shadows. And the smoke got thicker, stinging the eyes and choking the nose and throat.

People were cheering on the looters. Then, encouraged by their success, more people began to get in on the action, until, before long, everyone seemed to be running into blasted-out stores all along the street. I felt sick. Our own people were pillaging the heart of black Detroit. It was a sea of angry black faces.

We watched with a sick, stunned feeling as the carnage grew.

People were coming down from other 'hoods, and they began fighting over things. One guy crashed a liquor bottle over another guy's head, spraying glass, booze, and blood. Two or three jumped on him. Then a couple came to *their* rescue. Before you knew it, there was a crowd of women and men brawling in the middle of the street, fighting over looted goods. Others continued to break into shops all along 12th and the streets running off 12th.

To get back to the car, we had to fight against the crowd surging toward us like the tide of bodies after a sold-out concert or baseball game. Thousands were pouring into the area, and we were fighting against the flow to leave.

More sirens, more fires, more crashing glass, smoke, gunshots, explosions. People gone crazy! They were attacking one another. A mob of about forty young guys were yelling profanities and tossing bricks and beer bottles at passing cars, smashing in the windows.

We came upon a grey-haired man in his late sixties. He was slumped on the sidewalk, mumbling. He was drunk. I knelt down and had a look at him. It appeared he'd been ice-picked. His shirt was blood soaked from a wound in the upper right shoulder, but there was no cut, just a small hole, an entry wound. He'd caught either a bullet or an ice-pick. When switchblades were outlawed, ice-picks took their place as weapons. Maybe the old fellow had got in somebody's way. Maybe he'd tried to stop somebody from stealing. Or maybe he himself had been stealing. Whatever the case, when we came upon him, he looked up at me with terror in his eyes and put his hands up to cover himself, as if we had come to finish him off.

I said, "Hey, man, we ain't gonna hurt you. We gotta get you out of the way. You're hurt bad."

We dragged him to the other side of the street, where there was less activity, and set him in the protection of a doorway. More and more chaos was all around: glass crashing, screaming, explosions. But the old fellow waved us off to leave him alone. He probably wanted to get back into it, to get his share. So we moved on, but I often wondered if he made it or became one of the statistics of that night's forty-three dead.

We made it to the car, and I said to Rose, "I think we better get across to Ma's house tonight."

The Death of Blackbottom

We headed south along Trumbull, toward the tunnel, and we saw truckloads of Detroit police dressed in full battle dress: helmets, Plexiglas shields, body armour. And more and more police were being called in, until the streets were thick with blue uniforms. More fire trucks were coming in as well and more ambulances. Property was going up in flames all around us.

We tried to get to the tunnel, but it had been closed, and cars were backed up for miles. Then we got word on the radio that the Ambassador Bridge was also closed. The border to Canada was sealed, both the tunnel and the bridge. Detroit gas stations had been ordered closed. But that didn't slow down the bomb making. People could be seen all over downtown siphoning gas out of the tanks of cars along the street. With no way out, we decided to try to make it back to the north end, to the safety of Rose and Charlie's place.

We'd just turned back north on Trumbull when the cops

pulled us over. They had the bullhorns going: "Pull over! Pull over *now!*" They ordered us out. Two of them tore up the interior of the car looking for weapons. They didn't find any, so they turned on us. They ordered Charlie, TC, and me to lie facedown on the street.

TC said, "I ain't getting down, man. I ain't done nuthin' wrong."

"Get down now, nigger, or we'll blow your black ass away."

There was no question they were deadly serious. How many blacks had already been shot by police that night? We complied, but still everything was nigger this and nigger that. Detroit's finest at their worst. Big, mean, white bulls. They searched us, and TC had a straight razor on him. Straight razors weren't illegal, but they were deadly. Guys used to strop them so sharp that sometimes you didn't even feel it when you were sliced.

"Whaterya doing with this straight razor, nigger?"

"I gotta shave."

The cop kicked him in the ribs and whacked him on the side of the head with his nightstick.

I said, "Hey, man, leave him alone."

For that I caught a good thump on the side of the head from another cop.

An angry crowd of blacks started to gather, menacing the cops, calling them "racist pigs," spoiling for a confrontation. The cops got nervous and finally told us just to get the hell out of that part of town, which is what we were trying to do in the first place. We found out later that the jails were already filled to overflowing. They had no plans to arrest us; they just wanted to kick us around a bit. Maybe shoot us if we'd given them enough cause.

We set out again for Rose and Charlie's.

A few blocks north we were stopped again. Another police roadblock checking for weapons. People were rioting all around — busting windows, firing guns nearby, shooting and killing each other — but the cops did very little about it. We heard later they'd been given orders, at that point, to stay out of it unless attacked: "Let the property damage go. The situation's too hot." This stop was a brief one — a quick scan for guns, gas cans, and the like.

We got onto the John R. Lodge Expressway and headed north. Dawn was arriving, but flames could still be seen burning brightly from downtown. Cars were parked all along the John R., people leaning against them, standing in small clusters, sitting on hoods and trunks, just watching, staring in disbelief as Detroit burned. New fires were still sprouting up all over the downtown.

I was never so relieved to get home. When we stepped inside Rose and Charlie's house, we were pretty shook up. It was the worst night of my life, which is something to say considering some of the nights I'd been through. People were dying even as we walked in the door. People's homes and businesses were being destroyed by their friends, the very people they'd serviced and traded jokes with over the years.

As we walked in, the phone was ringing. It was Ma and Dad. They'd been watching everything from the other side of the river, standing on the porch, watching the Detroit skyline light up, hearing the explosions and the gunshots. They'd been phoning for hours, out of their minds with worry because we hadn't answered. When Rose grabbed up the phone, Ma was scared to death.

"Baby, what's going on? What's going on? Oh, it looks terrible. Terrible! Are y'all okay?"

We were okay, but black bottom was burning to hell.

We turned on the TV and watched the news reports in stunned silence. Shortly after that, there was a local news blackout of the riots, but for a while for the first time in America you could watch riots live on TV, like a ball game in progress. People were out in the streets talking about it at five in the morning. No one could sleep.

We heard the National Guard had now been called in, and gunshots were still popping everywhere, homemade bombs were booming, sirens were rising and falling. Mixed in now were chopper blades whirring, tanks clanking, tires screeching, people screaming, smoke and sparks filling the sky. People just arriving from downtown brought stories of new horrors: "Oh, lord, they're killing each other. It's terrible. Awful."

The day after the riot, I awoke and said to myself, "Once and for all, I'm getting away from this anger. This hatred. This hostility. This ignorance. This *insanity*."

But for the next four days, we were trapped.

The second and third days were even worse than the first.

Even with reinforcements, the National Guards couldn't gain control of the city. "Burn, baby, burn!" became the catchphrase of the riot, made famous by Black Panther cofounder H. Rap Brown, and it resonated around old Detroit like a death chant. Most of what burned was black occupied and burned out by blacks. We had turned inward and torn ourselves apart. How badly must you hate something — hate yourself — to want it to burn? It's what too

Foolishly, on night three of the riot I was drawn back downtown by some perverse fascination. Even more people were on the rampage. The smell of gasoline floated down every street — 12th, Trumbull, Beaubien, Brush, Buchanan — mixing with the stench of smoke and burnt cordite from gunfire.

And now you also had snipers on the roofs and at windows. Angry brothers wanting to get even and taking potshots at the National Guards and the police. Authorities fired back, not always with the most precision, raking entire building fronts and rooftops with heavy automatic weapons fire. More people were dying.

On Trumbull, I saw four black guys lying facedown on the street with Guardsmen standing over them, bayonets to their backs. More bodies were lying along the street. Corpses. It made you sick to see them. One was that of a kid, maybe sixteen. Women nearby, probably parents or relatives, were screaming and spitting at the Guardsmen, only teenagers themselves recruited into action from homes far away from the insanity.

Some of the baddest cats from some of the toughest 'hoods went downtown to do some shopping. Some actually had lists: one stereo, one TV, a case of bourbon, a couple of good new suits. These people, as casually as they may have acted, knew that they were risking their lives if police or store owners got a shot at them, and if you got in their way they'd have blown you away without a thought.

A pick-up truck pulled up to a blasted-out furniture store, and two men carried out a huge entertainment section — a wall unit with TV, hi-fi, and speakers all built in. Then they loaded on a couple of more TVs and hi-fis and drove away as if it was just another evening's shopping.

And there was plenty of liquor flowing. Liquor stores were among the first to get hit. And the more people drank, the drunker and crazier they got. Every bootlegger in the city had someone downtown collecting liquor for him.

People who weren't stealing were yelling encouragement and even helpful comments: "Man, you missed that one over there." That sort of thing.

Young punks were torching parked cars. I saw a group of guys running along, smashing in car windows, tossing in a bottle of gas, throwing in a match, and watching the car go up in flames. There were cars and trucks burning along many streets, almost all black owned.

For some folks, it was like the TV show in which you have only so many minutes to fill your shopping cart before the buzzer goes off. For others, it was like a stroll with friends. I saw women in curlers pushing loaded shopping carts down the centre of the street side by side as if they were walking down the aisle of the grocery store, except they were headed home. The National Guards eventually sealed off many of the stores not completely burned to the ground, but before they got into place people were loading up, running back home, unloading, and then racing back for more. People were warehousing goods in their living rooms, closets, bedrooms. For the first time in their lives, some people had televisions, hi-fi sets, new clothes, new furniture, and lots of food.

Other people were crying. You could hear their sobs. They regretted it. They could see the horror of self-destruction going on, and they knew that it would never be the same, that Detroit would never be the same.

By the third day, there were running gun battles between looters and police. You could hear the helicopters overhead, sighting people for the cops below. Some battles were intense, going back and forth for prolonged periods. Especially when the cops pinpointed a shooter from a building.

The 101st Airborne, just back from Vietnam, occupied Detroit's downtown east side, and the Michigan State Guard took over the west side. From everywhere you could hear the mechanical squawk of bullhorns, soldiers from atop tanks addressing the crowds: "Leave the area — now. Evacuate the area — now."

It's scary seeing a big old U.S. Army tank clanking its way down the centre of a city street toward you. The tank rattled past, and the sidewalk shook. I caught a good look at the Guardsmen, three young white boys and a seasoned white sergeant chomping down on a cigar. Probably a 'Nam veteran. The boys looked wild-eyed and scared, but that big sergeant looked mean and maybe even a little glad to be there, champing at the bit to get his baton on a black neck.

One guy who died during the riots was a dude name Rollie, who hung out at Bumps' place. Rollie got it on the third day. In the back. He was one of the leaders of the parade of looters. He was bad, and he always attracted too much attention. This time Rollie caught a bullet. It was never determined who had fired it. He apparently stayed a long time on the ground before anyone came for him.

A cousin called up to tell us that a couple of other dudes I knew had also been murdered. The two had gone cruising the Grand River area the first night to make a drug buy, maybe not even aware just how bad the rioting had become. Instead of drugs, they had found some rioters who'd shot both of them dead, taken their money, moved their bodies into the back seat of the car, sprinkled gasoline inside, and thrown in a match. When their charred remains were found, one had a knife in his back. That's what the dark side of the 'hood was like.

We didn't go downtown after the third day. It was too sickening. And it got so that, with stray bullets zinging everywhere, it wasn't safe even to watch.

By the fifth day, the riots had finally run themselves out, and the border to Canada reopened.

I set out right away for Windsor. On the way, along the shoulders of the John R., big military trucks and tanks were still grouped. I arrived across the border into Windsor, back at my parents' small house.

The next morning, before dawn, I slipped out of bed while my family was still sleeping, and I went down to the river. The sun was just coming up, a red shimmering ball in the east, but it was already hot and sticky, soon to be another blistering day. I pulled out the little .32-calibre snub-nosed Bulldog that I had tucked into my belt at my backside. I'd kept that gun with me for years. It made me feel safer. It was so compact and chunky, yet it slipped out of sight and stayed where you tucked it. I looked at it closely. The gunmetal had a seductive bluish tinge, and the handgrip was a dark solid wood. It felt like a real fine piece of machined weaponry, even if it was in reality a cheap Saturday Night Special. I'd always taken pride in it. I'd polished it and cleaned it on occasion. But now I wanted nothing to do with it. Now it just seemed like another false trapping of a dangerous and treacherous lifestyle.

I popped open the cylinder. Six brass shells with ugly little lead tips dropped into my hand. Fondling the bullets used to give me a feeling of power and security, safety from harm. Now they just gave me the creeps. I cupped them in my hand, drew my arm back, and flung them as far into the murky Detroit River as I could. They stayed airborne for several seconds, then splashed into the water in a pattern of little plops.

Then I took the Bulldog and did the same. I grabbed it by the barrel for leverage and tossed it in a big arcing motion, kind of like a discus thrower. It also seemed to hang suspended for several seconds in the clear air and then dropped into the brown water. It too disappeared in a hollow plop.

For several minutes, I stood there in silence and stared across the river at the still-smouldering skyline of Detroit. I knew straight up that, if I was ever to make it in this life, it couldn't be by living in that hell hole. Something was happening within me, something was speaking to my heart. I no longer felt that youthful immortality that had got me through so many past battles. That morning I felt fortunate just to be alive.

Years before a dream had been born and then died in my heart. I'd buried that dream so many years ago I'd almost convinced myself it hadn't been important. Now memories of that dream came back. The dream had been to *become* something in life. Become a *somebody*. I decided that day by the bank of the Detroit River to revive that dream and to dedicate myself to making it come true.

I went back home, threw a few things into a paper shopping bag, and that morning left my parents' home in

Windsor, jumped a bus down to the 401, and began hitch-hiking east to Toronto. I had only $3.35 in my pocket, and it grieved me to turn my back on Detroit this final time, a place I loved, but the black heart of Detroit was gone.

Now so was I. I was leaving for good the land of overt bigotry and heading back to the masters of subtle racism.

Running with the Panthers

CHAPTER 22

Back in Toronto, I couldn't leave behind some of my old ways.

About a month after I returned, I was arrested for taking part in a brawl at a dance. Just like when I'd gone back to Windsor earlier, when the police discovered outstanding warrants against me, I was held until my Monday-morning court appearance. When Monday morning rolled around, the judge laid a two-hundred-dollar fine or sixty days in jail on me. Two hundred dollars was out of the question, so I was hauled back in a paddy wagon to the Don Jail, where they forced me to give up my street clothes for jailhouse attire.

One night, about two weeks into my sentence, just before lockdown, a guard relayed a message to me that a friend had called and said he was going to make my bail. I rushed around promising my fellow inmates all kinds of favours when I got outside.

After lights went out, I sat on the edge of the cot eagerly

awaiting my freedom. About an hour later, a booming voice from the front hollered, "Jones, you've made bail! Toss out all your clothes, including your underwear, into the middle of the corridor. Pillow and sheets included."

"Hot dog!" I thought. "I'm checking out of this cockroach paradise."

I peeled off every stitch of clothing, pulled the sheets and pillow off the bed, and tossed them through the bars. Then I sat in that cold, damp cell, naked as the day I was born, waiting for the screw to set me free.

It never happened! I had no clue I'd been set up for an old jailhouse prank until the snickers and wisecracks told me I'd been had! It was an old joke played on all the new fish. A guy in the first cell had pretended to be the guard. I was never bailed out. I sat buck naked that night and ended up doing the entire sixty days.

One night, not long after I got out, I was sitting in an after-hours joint run by my cousin Joe Patterson called the Four Brothers Club. It was a place where the fast-lane set congregated to gamble and party till dawn. About one that morning, in waltzed Diana Ross, Mary Wilson, and Cindy Birdsong in Flo Ballard's place — the current Supremes. They'd just done their show at the O'Keefe Centre. Cousin Joe escorted them directly over to our table, and the place erupted into a feeding frenzy of autograph seekers.

After the commotion settled down, Joe ordered drinks, and when Mary Wilson discovered that I'd lived in Detroit we began to reminisce about the good old days. As teenagers, we used to frequent a lot of the same places, like the Greystone Ballroom and the Arcadia Roller Rink. Next thing I knew we were out on the floor dancing. Man, could she kick it!

As for Diana Ross, she was aloof and didn't talk much. I was tempted to remind her about the time my Galahads had won first place over her Primettes in the talent contest years before, but I didn't because she seemed to have things on her mind. It was only a few months after that night that she left the Supremes to embark on her solo career. I'll say this for her, though: when she got up to dance, she was one of the smoothest women I've ever danced with. Man, she moved around the floor like a gazelle. She never smiled or said much, just danced.

About that time, I hooked up with another old music acquaintance, Ronnie Hawkins, the legendary Arkansas rockabilly star who'd moved to Toronto and owned a nightclub in town called Le Coq D'Or Tavern. I'd first met Ronnie in George Chuvalo's dressing room after Chuvalo's bout with Ali in 1966. Hawkins had told me to stop by sometime at the gym where he worked out. After my stint in the Don, I did stop by to see him. An old guy named Whitey picked up an acoustic guitar lying around the gym, and began strumming out "Stormy Monday Blues." I jumped in and began singing and Hawkins heard me, and the next thing I knew we were jamming together, and he invited me down to Le Coq D'Or for a jam session.

The afternoon I dropped by, Eddie Floyd was playing there. Eddie had a huge hit the year before with the R&B classic "Knock on Wood." I'd just won the Canadian Golden Gloves Light-Heavyweight Championship Tournament the night before at the Paul Sauvé Arena in Montreal, and, with my victory in the sports pages of the Toronto papers that morning, I was feeling pretty good.

Hawkins swung by my table to congratulate me on my

win and asked me to come up and do a set with him. I yelled for Eddie Floyd to come on up and join me, and, between the three of us, we had the place in a strong groove.

When I'm entertaining, sometimes I get caught up in the music like folks do at revival meetings. It's a spiritual thing. In gospel music, they call it getting slain by the spirit. Halfway through the tune, I yanked my suit coat off and flung it away. Then I jumped back from the mike, cut loose, and did the splits twice, which brought the crowd to its feet. Man, I had it going on! But when I came up from the second splits, the whole crowd was laughing and pointing at me. Then I heard a voice from behind me holler, "Spider Jones got an asshole full of soul!" I looked over my shoulder, and there was Eddie Floyd on his knees, in hysterics. That's when I felt the breeze. I looked down, and there — exposed to the world — dangled my family jewels. I'd split the ass out of my pants, and I wasn't wearing any underwear! That morning I'd taken a shower and discovered that I had no clean shorts. I guess you could say I showed 'em that I had a lot of balls. I also shattered the myth that all black men are well hung!

I was back living at Sully's, and shortly afterward I became a member of the Black Panthers Party when an older friend of mine named Howard dropped by Sully's and told me about how he'd been hanging out in Oakland with the Panthers. The brothers had really fired him up. So much so that he wanted to form a local chapter in Toronto, and he wanted me to be the first member.

Once I joined, Howard and I began a recruiting campaign. We hit the pool halls, bars, clubs, and street corners. Eventually, we ended up with about twenty recruits. Howard appointed me the minister of warfare, which was ironic considering that was the title I'd held with my gang.

My duties included teaching members hand-to-hand combat, and we didn't have to wait long to use it. One Friday night I was just about to leave my crib when the phone rang. It was Snake, another party member. "You better get over here to Howard's place real fast!" I tried to prod him for details, but all I got was dial tone.

When Howard opened his door, the left side of his face was so badly swollen his eye had closed, and he was covered with dried blood.

"What the hell happened?" I asked.

"Why they want to beat up on me?" he sobbed. "I never did them no wrong!"

"Who did this?"

He didn't answer, just cried.

Over his shoulder, I caught a glimpse of Snake lying on the couch. His face was also a swollen mess.

It took an hour for Howard to settle down enough to explain what had happened. He and Snake had been downtown recruiting when they'd been approached by a group of skinheads.

"One of those son of a bitches snatched my beret. When I chased after him to get it back, some other dude wearing a Confederate army cap turned and sucker-punched me in the face."

While he was down, they put the boots to him. Snake rushed to his defence, and they jumped him too and used his head for a dance floor. Then they kicked on Howard a few more times while hollering racial slurs.

Over the past few months, the skinheads had been

throwing a lot of boot parties in Toronto. There was no choice but to track down Howard's assailants and do a little skinhead downsizing, so during the next few weeks we hit the clubs, bars, and restaurants in the downtown area where we figured the assailants hung out. All we got was graveyard silence. Nobody knew a thing.

Then Howard and I dropped into the Brown Derby, where the guy who managed the joint — former Canadian welterweight champion Sammy Luftspring — had eyes and ears in the clubs, on the streets, and in the alleys. When something needed to be found out, he was the man. He promised to put out some feelers.

A few days later, Howard phoned. "Sammy just called. Does the name Tex mean anything to you?"

I thought it over for a few seconds, trying to recall where I'd heard the name. Then it hit me — Tex was a big, gap-toothed piece of trash who always wore a Confederate army cap. I'd had a run-in with him a few months back.

I'd been chilling out with a white fox named Laura when she came up with the bright idea of dropping by the Gerrard House, a bar where tough, working-class white guys hung out. Bad idea! We walked in, and one guy in particular, a lanky, tough-looking kid with a peeled head and a Confederate cap, kept looking me up and down, fronting me off, trying to bait me into a fight. Over the next hour, the tension became too much, and I couldn't sit still. Finally, after struggling to keep my cool, I decided it would be best to leave. I told my date I was going to hit the can, and then we'd finish our drinks and cut out for my crib.

In case they followed me to the washroom, I reached into my pocket and pulled out a small cellophane bag that contained a mixture of cayenne pepper and sand. I poured most of the contents of the bag into my right hand and then closed it into a fist.

When I returned to the table, I noticed my date's eyes were teary. "What's up? Why are you crying?" She didn't reply. Then I noticed a small message card lying next to her purse, the kind that generally accompanies a bouquet of roses. We were in the beer hall section. Someone must have gone and snatched a long-stemmed rose from the front lounge area. I picked up the card: *Roses are red, violets are blue, you're a tramp and a nigger lover too.*

That blew it! I grabbed the rose and flew over to Tex's table, and I smacked Tex across the face with the long thorny stem. It left a big, ugly red welt on his cheek. He reached for me, and I moved back half a step and flung the pepper and sand straight into his eyes. He screamed and fell to the ground, rolling around like he was having a fit. One of his boys jumped out of his chair, and I snatched a beer bottle off the table and smashed it upside his head. He too sagged to the floor, blood spurting out of him like a fountain. I was just about to move in to finish Tex off when two bouncers came charging into me like tanks. I'd have been in big trouble except the head bouncer was Baldy Chard — fortunately somebody I knew — and he ordered everyone to back off.

I later heard that Tex had spent the night in the hospital getting the sand dug out of his eyes. So you could say there was already a good hatred between us.

"Sammy says this is our man!" Howard said. "He's been bragging at the Gerrard House how he kicked the shit out of a couple of niggers up on Yonge Street. And he's been showing off my beret too!"

"How many guys we got ready to go?" I asked.

"Four. Five, counting me," he said and rattled off their names.

I almost dropped the phone. These guys were pussies. Not one of them knew how to fight. "Damn, Howard!" I yelled, "you wanna bring hip shakers to a bone-breaker's party?"

I thought about the Golden Glove tournament I had coming up the following Friday night. I was running low on cash, and the tournament would be a chance to pick up a few extra dollars on side bets. The last thing I needed was to bust my hands up on some fool's hard head. I also knew that Howard was dead set on revenge and that, with or without me, he intended to confront these guys. Loyalty prevailed.

"Okay, I'm on the way," I told him.

We rounded up the others, and as we drove toward the Gerrard House there was a nervous silence among us. I studied the faces, saw fear in their eyes. These guys had joined the Panthers because it was trendy. Now the game was heading in a violent direction, and they'd be forced to fight. Howard was the only game one among them. Question was how a middle-aged man who smoked a pack of cigarettes a day and drank whisky like it was water could deal with a pack of vicious skinheads.

The closer we got to the Gerrard House, the more I realized how dangerous the confrontation was going to be. I had to come up with a plan, and an idea popped into my head — Baldy Chard. Baldy was as stocky as a bull and had biceps as thick as most men's legs; at five foot nine and 235 pounds, he was built for battle. He was considered the toughest street fighter in Toronto. The Gerrard House was his turf, and only a damn idiot would waltz in there looking for trouble and face Baldy. That's when it came to me! Baldy loved a good fight. Even more, he loved to gamble on fights. In fact, that's how we first became acquainted a few years earlier.

I was competing in a Golden Gloves tournament, which turned into a pretty dirty affair. There were a lot of foul shots and hitting on the breaks and after the bell. It got so bad that midway through the third round the referee stopped the bout and was about to disqualify both of us when this stocky bruiser with a brush cut charged into the ring like a rogue elephant. He was mad as hell and shook his fist at the referee as if he wanted to kill him. He said he had money riding on the fight, and he didn't want to hear any talk of disqualification. The poor ref was so scared he almost took off right out of the ring. In the end, he relented and allowed the fight to continue. My trainer leaned over and said with a touch of awe, "That's Baldy Chard." I understood then why the referee was so intimidated. I'd heard Baldy's name many times before.

After the fight, Baldy came charging into my dressing room along with another stocky guy dressed in a flashy, two-piece gabardine suit and puffing on a big cigar. "Nice fight, kid," Baldy grinned and slapped me on the back. It blew me away to have the man known as the King of Cabbagetown stroking my ego. "I'm Baldy Chard," he said, "and this here is my partner, the Weasel."

The Weasel, whose real name was Marv Elkind, looked like a heavy from a *Godfather* film. I later learned that Marvin had been personal chauffeur to some heavy-duty dudes, including Jimmy Hoffa, Sonny Liston, and Joe Frazier. He asked me if I needed some dough, and, before I could answer, he laid a ten spot on me and told me not to worry about paying it back, because they'd won a good chunk betting on me. Strictly speaking, in order to keep our amateur status, we weren't supposed to take money, but under-the-table "bonuses" were accepted all the time. After that, Baldy and the Weasel showed up at a lot of my fights and always laid a little coin on me afterward. Not once did they ask for anything in return, except that I put in a good fight.

The Weasel often insisted that if I ever needed anything I could call him. Now the moment of truth had arrived, and I wondered whether he was on the square or just giving lip service. He answered on the first ring.

"Weasel, it's Spider. I need you to do something for me real bad and right away. There might be some dough in it for you."

"What's doing?" he asked.

"I'm in front of the Gerrard House. I want you to approach Baldy and set up a fight between Tex and me, inside the hotel, after hours."

The prospect of making some dough on a fight bet put the Weasel onside right away. "I'll call Baldy," he said.

Ten minutes later I called back. "Baldy's in. We show up a half hour after closing time."

Smokin' Tex

We arrived at the hotel just after twelve-thirty, and Baldy greeted us at the front door.

"You ready to rumble, kid?" he asked, putting his beefy hand on my shoulder.

I nodded.

"Follow me."

He ushered us toward the back of the hotel. The place was gloomy and reeked of stale smoke and booze. To me, the scent of hostility was also thick in the air. It gave me the creeps. The only consolation I had was Baldy's word that nobody would interfere. But at the same time, I knew that I was in hostile territory and that I had to deal with an Aryan nut case, and there was no guarantee I'd survive him.

We shouldered our way to the back of the hotel through the crowd, most of whom had been boozing all night and were in a bloodthirsty state of mind. Somebody hollered,

"I've got ten dollars says Tex is going to punch out this spook kid real quick!"

I stared into the sea of hostile faces looking for Tex, and Baldy must have read my mind, because he tapped me on the shoulder and pointed toward the back. "He's in the kitchen warming up."

We arrived at an area where the chairs and tables had been cleared away. Baldy looked at me, pointed, and shouted so everyone could hear, "This is your ring, kid; prepare for battle!"

I began moving around like I was prepping for a sanctioned match — firing left jabs, right crosses, and hooks to limber up.

The crowd howled and hooted. "Hey, spook," somebody called out, "you look good fighting air."

I let it slide, determined to keep focused on the task at hand. I noticed, while moving around, that the floor was slippery. Somebody must have mopped it earlier. I'd been involved in enough barroom brawls to know that when you're fighting on a wet floor it's difficult to get traction from hard-soled shoes. Fortunately, I was wearing the sneakers I'd trained in earlier that day, and they would give me a good grip on the floor. I was hoping that Tex would be wearing those big, heavy, skinhead boots of his, the ones with cleats on the heels. That way he couldn't get set to punch, and if he missed me he'd be off balance, which would allow me to counterpunch. That was providing he didn't put those big boots to me first.

I spotted Tex before he saw me. He came strutting out of the kitchen flanked by four lackeys who were patting him on the back and stroking his ego. The sight of him sent a surge of adrenaline through my body, the same feeling I experienced heading into smokers. I had the feeling he was one of those crazy dudes who'd rush in swinging and attempt to overpower an opponent. I also knew that once we got going my emotions would settle down, and I'd get into a groove. First I'd have to weather a storm.

He was wearing his trademark Confederate cap and a cocky grin, and he was a lot bigger than I'd recalled. He had one of those tall, lean, and rangy builds with broad shoulders and long, well-defined arms that were dangerous. My boxing instincts took over, and I began to assess him. My best chance to get to him was to fight out of a crouch and try to get underneath his long arms. That way I could work from the hip to the lip and maybe land some bombs upside his head.

When he spotted me, his face stiffened, and his eyes lit up with the fiendish glow of somebody who loved busting people up. Without any warning, he charged me, swinging with both hands, and it caught me off guard. I'd figured Baldy would lay down some ground rules before we got going, but it happened so fast that everybody was caught by surprise.

I slipped sideways and moved inside, catching him with a solid left hook to the gut. The force of the blow made him gasp for air. For a fraction of a second, I thought that it might be over quickly, but instead of wilting he fired back a volley of blows, none of which landed. I kept popping away at his face with my left jab and bobbing and weaving in and out of his firing range. I'd sparred with professionals, and my confidence was beginning to soar.

I danced back into close range and landed three solid left jabs. The last one caught Tex squarely on the tip of the nose, and his eyes began to water, and his nose started bleeding. "Hey, boy," I taunted him, "where's all that smoke you supposed to be bringing?" He didn't say anything, just fired a long, lazy left jab, but he was slow bringing it back to cover up, a cardinal sin in boxing, and I landed another heavy hook to the body and then fired a short right overtop that landed flush on his jaw. He was in trouble and began to retreat, and I was sure he was my meat now. I should have remembered this was a street fight, not a Golden Gloves tournament.

Suddenly, Tex grabbed the back of my head, and, before I could react, he shoved my head down and brought his knee up full force into my face. The blow caught me high on the forehead and sent shock waves through my body. It felt like a bomb had exploded in my skull. I had to buy time to clear my head and get my legs back under me. I tried to dance out of range and at the same time fire left jabs to keep him back so he couldn't land the big adios, but my legs felt like overcooked spaghetti.

Tex stormed me, unleashing a rain of blows. One landed flush on my chin. My knees buckled, and I almost went down. The only thing that kept me up was pride. I was hurt and fighting on pure instinct. He swung another haymaker, one of those roundhouse punches you can see coming a mile away, and somehow I managed to duck it. He'd swung with such force that he lost his balance and slipped to the floor, which gave me a few extra seconds to recuperate.

Once my head began to clear, I quickly assessed Tex. His gut was heaving, his nostrils were flaring, and his mouth was wide open, sucking wind. Fatigue was setting in on him. But the most telltale sign was the look in his eyes. They were

filled with confusion. He was like a lot of bullies I've known
over the years. They count on a quick sucker punch to win.
The rest of their game is intimidation. If the sucker punch
can't get it done, then they've got nothing going. I may have
been physically smaller than him, but I was still a huge step
up in calibre for him.

Tex was desperate and running out of time. He'd blown
his big chance by letting me off the hook when he'd staggered me with the knee blow. The only chance he had now
was to land a lucky shot, but I moved in for the finish. It was
time to close the show.

He tried to keep me off with a right hand, but I slipped
under it, moved to the side, and rammed an elbow into his
ribcage. He screamed and doubled up. I brought the same
elbow up into his chin. He staggered backward like a drunk.
"Welcome to the world of smokers," I thought, looking into
his glassy eyes. I threw a left to his jaw and then slammed the
heel of my sneaker full force into the side of his knee. I could
feel it snap. He let out a cry of agony and dropped to the
floor. He tried to get up, but he fell over helplessly on his
back. With his knee gone and his nose broken, Tex was done.
He was at my mercy, and I could have done to him what he'd
done to Howard and Snake, but something within wouldn't
let me do it.

I looked over at Howard, and he nodded toward the
door. It was over. I collected my bets from Baldy and left.
Word of the fight got out, and we never had any more trouble with the skinheads.

As time progressed, I began to realize that, for me, being a
member of the Panthers was more about power-tripping

than anything else. If you were into fox hunting, being a Panther was a big perk. The ladies dug our apparel, which consisted of a black beret, black T-shirt, black shades, and black three-quarter-length leather jackets. I'd be out there fronting big-time, acting like I was some kind of soldier of fortune, swaggering into dances, nightclubs, and restaurants, showboating like a big-time player. There'd be all kinds of flirtatious compliments and other stuff going on with the girls. I knew it was more about the uniform than about me.

I had some super times with the Panthers. The best thing was that I really got schooled on the black man's plight in a white-ruled corporate world. On a few occasions, we travelled to Detroit and Chicago and even to Oakland for a big rally there, where I got to hear legendary Panther founder Bobby Seale speak.

Bobby was one of the most electrifying speakers I've ever heard. He took me to school on how blacks and other minorities were being oppressed by a racist system. He spoke with a burning passion about how the system was brutalizing and dehumanizing blacks. I'd seen it and lived it, but his message spoke directly to my heart. It also gave me a better understanding of why we as blacks were so angry. He was a man who had the courage to call America what it was: an oppressive, racist system that kept blacks at the bottom of the barrel, living in poverty not by choice but by design.

Being in Oakland and hanging out with Bobby and other prominent Panthers made me feel like a big dog, especially when Howard introduced me as the minister of warfare for the Toronto chapter.

After the rallies, there'd always be a party thrown by the

host city. We'd hang out, sip on wine, and talk about how we
were going to bring justice and equality to "the people."
Once in Chicago, I was asked to get up and testify to a crowd
of about two hundred people about what the Black Panther
Party meant to me. Being the son of a preacher man, along
with all my Southern Baptist nurturing, testifying came nat-
urally to me. I jumped up to the podium breathing fire and
yelling "Power to the people!" I told how, before I joined the
Panthers, I was out in the streets acting like a chump, fighting and going to jail, how the Panthers had given me
motivation and a new perspective on life, all the while
pounding the podium like I'd seen Reverend C.L. Franklin
do at the New Bethel Baptist years earlier. "Brothers and sisters, we must devote *and even sacrifice ourselves* to the
struggle to attain the equality our people have been so long
denied!" Man! I was blowing smoke, woofin' it up, and putting on a show. The brothers and sisters were all fired up.
They were hollering back all kinds of encouraging words as
if we were at a Sunday-night revival meeting. When I finished, they gave me a standing ovation.

I also learned firsthand that the Panthers were not the
barbarians the media of the time depicted them to be. To go
by some of the media, they were a bunch of rowdy-assed
niggers out to murder white folks. This was a myth created
by deceitful factions of a treacherous U.S. propaganda
machine trying to torpedo the movement. The negative
press is understandable when you consider that most of the
media at the time were predominantly white. Most still are.
Many have had little contact with blacks of the inner cities
and the projects. It was because of these kinds of misin-
formed media "authorities" that the apathetic American

public was fed a negative, one-sided diet of Panther bad press. False reports were often provided by the FBI.

It was J. Edgar Hoover who also fabricated lies about Martin Luther King and wiretapped his home, office, and travel stops looking to get dirt on him. Hoover viewed both King and the Panthers as part of a communist threat. Consequently, when people read the papers, or saw highlights on the evening news of the bloody confrontations between the cops and the Panthers, they assumed the Panthers had initiated the trouble. Even now few know the truth about the acts of compassion they performed.

On one occasion, I was at a rally in Chicago with H. Rap Brown when I spotted a couple of white kids at one of the breakfast programs. Out of curiosity, I asked him why the party was feeding white kids. The dude looked me straight in the eye and said that the program was about feeding hungry kids, regardless of colour. As a black person, it filled me with great pride to be associated with such compassion. To Brown, like Bobby Seale, the Panther movement was a labour of love. He didn't give a damn what colour a hungry kid was.

During visits to other American cities, I also witnessed Panthers feeding whites, Chicanos, Native Americans, and any other kids who came looking for a meal. You never heard much about *that* in the media, though.

Sure, there were some renegades among the Panthers — such is life in any organization — but for the most part they were proud black men who'd grown angry at and tired of being accused, misused, and abused by a racist system. Tired of seeing their baby brothers and sisters end up as corpses in the ashes of bombed-out churches. Tired of seeing the Klan lynching their boys. Tired of seeing white Americans getting the gravy while tossing them a few leftovers. As far as I'm concerned, all Afro-North Americans owe a huge debt to the Panther movement, many of whom sacrificed their lives to make things better for us.

Even though being a Panther was an exciting experience, after a few months I began to grow disillusioned. I became tired not of what the Panther Party stood for but of defending the loudmouthed, fake-assed Panthers of our Toronto branch. Most of them couldn't lick a postage stamp if you stuck it on their lips, yet they were always getting up in somebody's face. A lot of them were using the movement to exploit their hatred of whites. It seemed we were constantly getting into brawls and confrontations over petty crap. Being the minister of warfare, I was expected to come to the rescue of any careless brother who swam in over his head. Most of them were on personal ego trips and didn't give a damn about tarnishing the Panther image, nor did they have the slightest clue how special the Panthers had become to much of the black community. All the unnecessary brawling and threatening served to do was substantiate the media-perpetuated myth that the Black Panthers were a gang of white-hating warmongers.

I had many white friends who'd been right by me, so all that hollering about killing whitey and other stuff wasn't cool with me. The Panthers were serious business, and you had to be committed body and soul to be a good one. I respected them too much to keep playing the ego game. So I moved on.

About that time, I got a call one morning from boxing promoter Vince Bagnato asking me if I was up for playing a sparring partner in a movie called *Title Contender*, to star Tony Curtis. Being unemployed, I jumped all over it.

The next morning I was tossed in the ring with some well-muscled brother and told to make the scene look as realistic as possible. The director stressed that he wanted a heated session, so, following his cue, I went right after my opponent and began pounding away, expecting that he could defend himself. However, within a few seconds, I realized the only ring he'd ever seen was the one around his collar. The director panicked and rushed into the ring frantically yelling "Cut! Cut!"

He pulled me aside and said that in this particular scene the actor was portraying the heavyweight champion of the world training for a big fight. "And you're making him look like chopped liver!" he wailed. I got the message and agreed to go easy and attempt to make the guy look good. But it didn't work. His timing was so bad he couldn't portray a poodle, let alone a boxer. Following a few more futile attempts, I suggested to the frustrated director that he shoot around the scene and allow me to tutor his kid for a few days. He bought the idea.

I spent the next few days working on his left jab, right hand, footwork, and balance. He was a good athlete and caught on fast. The director was so pleased that he hired me on the spot to assist Bagnato in coordinating the boxing and fight scenes.

The next morning, while we were sparring, I heard a voice boom out, "Nice moves, fellas!" There, to my surprise, standing on the ring apron all decked out in a white suit and Chicago-style Stetson was the man himself — Tony Curtis. At noon, the director called a lunch break, and Curtis called me to join him, and we had a great time discussing boxers and past great fights.

One afternoon one of the crew asked me what I was up to that evening, and I mentioned that I'd be rolling by the Colonial Tavern later to catch a group I knew out of Detroit called the Dramatics. Curtis overheard and asked if he could tag along. "Please!" I told him. "It would be an honour."

That evening I picked him up at his hotel, and we hit the club. When we walked in, there was a funny delayed reaction. People looked over but weren't sure it was really Curtis. This was at a time when few movies were shot in Toronto, and nobody expected stars to walk in. Once it sunk in that he was indeed Curtis, the place broke into bedlam. He may not have been as hot as he was in the 1950s, but the women were still all over him like bees on honey.

Over the next few weeks, I acted as his chauffeur, guide, and security guy. It was one cool gig.

In those days, I also made an occasional buck hiring out as a sparring partner. I probably faced tougher fighters sparring than I did in my Golden Gloves tournaments because the paid sessions were usually with big-league pros. Guys like Clyde Gray, the Canadian welterweight champ, and George Chuvalo.

Sparring with George especially was a scary gig. I was fast and lean, but I was still only about 175 pounds, while George weighed in at about 215 in those days. And this was a guy who'd been in the ring by that time with Muhammad Ali, Joe Frazier, George Foreman, and Floyd Patterson — the toughest guys in the world — and they couldn't make him blink. So what was a guy like me supposed to do? George was a guy you couldn't hurt no matter what you did to him. In our sessions, he'd work mostly on body shots — pounding me on the shoulders, on the arms, in the kidneys, in the belly — and many a night after George I dragged my butt home hurting all over.

One time both I and one of George's regular sparring partners, Paul Neilsen (ranked in the top ten of the heavyweight division in Canada at the time and considered a hot prospect), were supposed to show up at Sully's to spar with George. Teddy McWhorters slathered Vaseline up and down George's arms. George was wearing this sleeveless white T-shirt that really accentuated his big, bulging forearms and shoulder muscles, now all shiny with the Vaseline, and he was so menacing looking that he looked like he'd just walked out of a horror movie. And I was already not feeling too good about getting in the ring with him, mainly because he was getting closer to a big fight, and when George got close to a fight he got more dangerous than ever because he wanted to make sure his timing was bang on and his power was at the max.

Mercy! I was damn near crapping my pants just waiting for Neilsen to show up, because he was supposed to go first and maybe wear George down a little over a few rounds, when the phone rang. With one eye nervously locked on George and my palms already sweating, I went over and picked up the phone. It was Neilsen.

He said, "Spider, it's Paul. Tell George I can't make it today. I got the shits."

I could only shake my head as I looked over at George whaling away at the heavy bag to warm up, putting huge-fist-sized indents in the thick canvas, and I replied, "Man, I know *exactly* how you feel. I think I'm about to get the shits myself."

Neilsen did *not* enjoy sparring with George. Neither did I. Nobody did. *George was tough on you!* It was that simple.

CHAPTER 24

You Are Everything . . .

By 1974, I was still occasionally fencing hot goods but mostly I was clubbing the night away and finally working a respectable day job in the sales department of a small promotions firm. Plus I was boxing and burning the candle at both ends.

I was a member of a loose group of guys who called ourselves the Hounds. We'd get sharp and hit the nightclubs hunting for foxes. Sometimes we'd bet on who'd pick up a fox the quickest. The losers would have to buy the winner and his date drinks and dinner. It may sound braggadocio, but I seldom had to reach into my kick. Nine out of ten times, I came through first. I was a good talker.

My days of dogging around spawned two semi-serious relationships. Both were attractive and intelligent ladies who had much to offer, but I had too much dog in me to do right by either of them. Living in poverty and seeing my parents in a constant struggle to make ends meet had jaded my perspective on marriage, family, or any other type of commitment. I saw myself as a player, and no woman was going to get my nose open till I was ready. That's what I thought.

Then it happened! Love at first sight hit me with the force of a runaway tractor-trailer.

"Hey, Spider," one of the guys I worked with shouted one day as he rushed into my office. "You've got to come downstairs and see the dynamite chick."

Downstairs was the lounge on the first floor where most of our staff congregated during lunch and after work.

"It takes a lot of dynamite in a woman to blow me away," I shrugged.

"Hey, man, this one's got it all going on."

I knew he was calling me out. Whenever a new lady came by the lounge, I was expected to roll on through and lay some game on her.

Truth was I didn't really feel up to it. Getting booty was no big deal to me. In fact, most of the time I got more by accident than most guys did trying. Another reason I wasn't too eager about going downstairs was because I was in training for an upcoming Golden Gloves bout, and I generally abstained from sex before a fight. The last thing I needed to deal with was temptation.

"Forget it," I told myself. "I'm going to the gym and then straight home."

I finished my reports and was about to leave when something compelled me to go downstairs: whispers, not so much in my head as in my heart. I know now that it was the hand of fate guiding me toward my destiny. Little did I suspect that my prowling days were about to come to an abrupt end. That my life was about to change forever!

I strolled through the door and made my way to a table near the back where my friends were seated. I slid into an empty seat. "So, where's this fox you dudes been raving about?" I asked, looking around.

"She went to the washroom." My brother Barry smiled and winked at me. He was expecting big brother to shoot some smooth lines her way.

Barry was my younger brother, born a year after Dennis died. Because he was a few years younger, we had a close connection; in some ways, it was as if he took Dennis's place. Barry and I were always close, and as a kid, he tagged after me.

The conversation switched to my upcoming fight at the Martin Luther King North America Golden Gloves Tournament in Rochester, New York. It was a big tournament; there would be fighters from all over North America. The guys wanted to know whom I'd be fighting and what kind of condition I was in.

After sparring with Chuvalo over the past few months and absorbing some heavy punishment, I knew I was in top shape. Unlike Ali, who would joke and clown around, George was all business in the ring; you were constantly on edge and on your toes, moving, ducking, defending yourself. You learned to use every bit of that ring to survive.

I began breaking down my possible prospects in Rochester, and pretty soon I forgot the reason I was there.

Then a soft, gentle voice from behind me interrupted our conversation. "Excuse me."

I turned to see whom it belonged to, and leaning over my shoulder was this stunningly attractive face.

"You stole my seat," she said with a radiant smile.

Our eyes locked for a few brief seconds. Hers were amber

brown and sparkled with a captivating glint of mischief. My friend Paul introduced us. Her name was the same as one of my all-time heroes: Jackie Robinson. When we shook hands, the touch of her hand lit me up.

"H-hi" was all I managed to stammer.

My body began to react in mysterious ways. No woman had ever come close to turning this kind of heat up in me. It was like I'd been injected with some sort of love potion. A nonbeliever in the powers of love at first sight, I couldn't explain why my heart pounded so and why my legs turned rubbery.

She flashed me another stunning smile and then squeezed by me and took her chair. She had the warmest and most sincere-looking eyes I'd ever seen, but she didn't even give me a second glance. Man, my ego took a big blow from that! But I couldn't take my eyes off her.

First thing I noticed was the slender shape of her face. Then how white her skin was, smooth and exquisite like a porcelain doll. I was more attracted to women with olive and dark skin, but something about her fascinated me. In dating, I never got hung up on colour or culture.

Over the next few hours, I sat back and quietly observed her. The more I saw, the more enamoured I became. The way she threw her head back when she laughed. Her small lips and her narrow chin, which appeared so delicate yet so strong and proud. I wanted to smother her lips with a thousand kisses. Who was this woman? What was her story? Did she have a man?

When she was on the dance floor, the sensuous motion of her hips and bottom sent tingling sensations to every nerve in my body. The two-piece white pantsuit she wore revealed a perfectly curved shape. Watching her made my blood boil with desire. At the same time, it frightened me to death. Why was I so captivated by this strange woman whom I knew nothing about? Something kept urging me to dance with her. But I couldn't work up the nerve to ask her. I was too frightened that she would reject me. To be honest, had fate not intervened, I probably would have blown it.

As destiny would have it, she made the first move. "How come everybody's dancing but you?" she asked as she returned to her seat.

My heart actually fluttered at the sound of her voice. All kinds of thoughts raced through my mind. Why did she ask? Is she attracted to me? I wasn't sure how to respond without looking like a fool. "Are you asking me?" I shot back, trying to sound nonchalant.

She never said anything, just answered with a sassy smile.

I was desperate to keep the conversation alive. "I like dancing to the slow music more than the fast stuff," I said.

She smiled another of her beguiling smiles and just gazed at me as though reading my thoughts.

It was a new and confusing experience for a confident player like me. Still, I was desperate to get with her. I decided to slow down the rhythm of the place, so I went over and slipped the DJ a five spot and requested a slow tune.

I still remember the first tune we danced to: "You Are Everything and Everything Is You" by the Stylistics. To this day, whenever I hear the tune, I think of that night and how I kept slipping the DJ five bucks to play slow, romantic tunes so I could prolong the intimacy of those moments. It worked! We spent most of the evening slow-dancing. As the words of that first tune we danced to implied, in time she would become everything and more to me: my strength, my inspiration, and above all the one who helped to guide me out of the darkness.

The evening was magic, but it ended too quickly for me. I offered her a lift home, and most of the fifteen-minute drive was in silence. All the while, my mind was in high gear trying to come up with a way to prolong the evening. By the time we arrived at her doorstep, I still hadn't come up with any plan. No slick lines, no seductive moves. It was kind of weird. I was twenty-eight years old and had dated many beautiful women, yet I couldn't come up with one smooth line. But my instincts told me she was attracted to me.

We parked in the driveway of her building and sat in silence for a few minutes listening to my tape of the Stylistics once again sing "You Are Everything and Everything Is You."

"Never forget this tune," I said to her. "It's the first song we ever danced to."

As I spoke, our eyes locked. I leaned over and gently tilted her chin up and brought my lips down slowly to meet hers. After a few seconds, she began to respond. Her finger began to lightly stroke the back of my neck, and then she touched and caressed my face. Her touch made me quiver with passion. It was a sweet, lingering kiss, and I could feel our bodies trembling in unison.

The kiss lasted probably no more than thirty seconds. Then she laid her head on my chest, and we held hands and sat quietly listening to the music. I finally broke the silence. "Go," I nudged, gently pushing her out of the car.

As she passed in front of it, she waved and shot me that stunning smile. "Call me," she hollered.

My heart sank as I watched her disappear into the

building. A feeling of loneliness crept over me. "If this is
love," I thought, "then it sure is a confusing feeling."

That night sleep eluded me till the wee hours of the
morning, and when it finally arrived her face, her smile, her
touch filled my dreams. When I awoke and discovered I'd
only been dreaming, I became dejected. That day she domi-
nated my thoughts so badly that I couldn't concentrate on
my work. I kept reliving our kiss, which excited me to such
a degree that I became lightheaded.

"This is crazy!" I thought. "How can one woman, on one
night, have this kind of effect on me? Is it fate?" Being spiritual, I did believe that God brings people together. These
days I no longer attempt to ask why. I settled for the term
"divine intervention." A blessing from God.

That afternoon I packed work in early and headed down
to the lounge hoping to run into her. She wasn't there, and I
prayed silently that she'd show. I decided to hang around
and see if my prayer would be answered. I spotted my
brother with some of my associates at the back and went
over to them. I told him I had some business to take care of,
so he'd have to grab a lift home with one of the other guys.

We shot the breeze for a few minutes; then they began
asking me how I'd made out with the chick last night. "Did
you get the booty?" sort of questions. For some reason, I
resented them referring to her as a chick. "She's not a chick,"
I shot back. "She's a prime-time lady."

The guys split around ten o'clock, and I grabbed a stool
at the bar and nursed a glass of wine, hoping she would
eventually show. The place was full, and the dance floor was
crowded with couples moving to the rhythm of the disco
beat. It seemed like everybody but me was having a good

time. I sat there moping like a broken-hearted fool, staring at myself in a bar mirror. Every once in a while, I'd glance toward the front entrance, hoping she'd stroll in.

Around ten-thirty, I spotted Georgette, a gorgeous French Canadian girl I'd been dating off and on, enter the lounge. I turned my head the other way in an attempt to avoid eye contact. I was too miserable to be in a socializing mood. Then there was a tap on my shoulder. "Hi, sweetie," Georgette smiled. I tried to conceal my disappointment. She was a super fine lady and fun to be with. Well, up until the night before.

She lured me onto the dance floor and started coming on to me about going back to her crib. Any other time I'd have been all over the idea. But something mysterious had come over me. I was acting more like a pussycat than a hound. It was as though my testosterone had shut down. How else could I explain this foreign behaviour? I mean, here was this fox offering me all the goodies, and I was declining her invitation. I made up some flimsy excuse and cut out.

Over the next hour, I passed by Jackie's apartment building three times, each time debating whether to knock on her door. Thing was I didn't want to impose on her or, even worse, create an embarrassing situation. All kinds of thoughts raced through my mind. Maybe she already had a man. Yet the sweet and intimate kiss we'd shared the night before hinted otherwise. There'd been too much promise in it. Unless she was a good actress.

The thought of her being in another man's arms greatly disturbed me, and I kept reminding myself that her last words had been "Call me." That thought lifted my spirits some. But I'd forgotten to get her phone number.

When you're enamoured of someone, you do all kinds of
weird things. Like the next morning, during the twenty-
minute drive to work, I kept replaying "You Are Everything
and Everything Is You." I was acting like a lovesick adolescent.

Two days after we met, I went to the lobby of her building and got her apartment number from the mail slot and
sent her a dozen long-stem roses. The message I sent with
them read "The beauty of these roses pales in comparison
to yours. Thank you for the wonderful time, I really
enjoyed your company. Hope we can get together very
soon." At the bottom, I left both my work and home phone
numbers. This may sound lame, but it came straight from
my heart.

After that, every time I heard a phone ring, my heart
would race with anticipation. Did she receive the flowers?
Would she call me?

About four o'clock that afternoon, the receptionist
buzzed my extension. "A call for you, Spider, on line two."

I snatched up the phone. "Good afternoon, Spider Jones.
How can I help you?"

"Hi," the sweet voice said.

I recognized it instantly. "Hello yourself," I said, trying to
hide my emotions.

"Thank you for the roses. They're beautiful." Her soft,
soothing voice turned me on and made my heart flutter.
"The note was nice too. It made my day."

I tried to sketch an image of her in my mind, her sassy
brown eyes and the delicate lips. "Do you have any plans for
tonight?" I asked. "I'd like to take you to dinner."

"I'd love to," she replied. "But I'm already committed to
a previous engagement."

I tried to hide my disappointment. "How about meeting me for an early drink, then?"

There were a few seconds of silence, and I thought she was either pondering my offer or playing hard to get. Or she just plain didn't want to see me. A burst of desperation surged through me. I had to come up with something to persuade her to meet me, but I didn't want to come on too strong. "I need to see you tonight," I said, and then, before she could respond, I added, "Please! I want your advice on something important." Then I waited humbly for a reply.

"What time?" she asked.

I glanced at my watch. It was a few minutes past four. "How's six sound?"

She agreed, and we arranged to meet at the lounge.

I strolled into the lounge about five minutes late so I wouldn't appear to be too excited. I glanced around the room and spotted her before she did me. She was seated next to my brother and the other usual suspects from our office. The sight of her quickened my pulse. She was wearing a stylish blue mini dress. I was immediately attracted to her shapely legs. They were smooth and slender and so delectable looking, even more attractive than the other night.

I eased up silently behind her and kissed her lightly on the cheek. She gave me a warm smile and cheerful hello. Both her nearness and fragrant scent aroused me. I pulled a chair up and sat as close to her as possible and exchanged pleasantries and small talk with the rest of the table.

About fifteen minutes later, I took her by the hand and guided her over to a quiet table in the back corner.

"How much time are you going to allow me before you leave to be with this very fortunate man?" I asked.

She burst into laughter. "I have to leave around eight-thirty."

"Good! That gives me a couple of hours to change your mind," I said.

A smirk tilted the corners of her mouth, and her eyes sparkled with amusement. "You mentioned you needed my advice on a very important matter," she reminded me. Her gaze was penetrating and curious.

I wasn't sure what to say next. "Why is this happening?" I wondered. I'd never had a problem communicating with women in the past, and suddenly I was stuck with a case of verbal constipation. "Forget the bull," I told myself, "just play it straight with her."

"There's this very special lady who I can't stop thinking about," I said and looked into her eyes. I added, "I'm so strung out on her that I can't think straight anymore. The thing that bothers me the most about it is I don't know how she feels about me."

Something registered in her eyes, as though she was trying to read me, to see if I was being for real or just trying to seduce her. After a few seconds of silence, she said, "Is it anybody I know?" She said it coyly, but something in her smile told me it was all good.

I placed my arm around her waist and pulled her to me. "You know exactly who it is, don't you?" I whispered in her ear.

"You hardly know me." The look in her eyes spelled uncertainty. She was still trying to figure me out. See if I was sincere about all these things I was saying.

"I know this much," I whispered. "No one in my life has ever moved me the way you do. I think fate has guided us together." And I was completely sincere when I told her that.

She stared at me for a few seconds and then broke into a beguiling smile. "You're smooth," she said, and we both laughed.

We talked, laughed, and shared stories over the next hour. I learned that she was a twenty-four-year-old divorced mother of two. She was working in the promotions department of an advertising firm and taking some evening school courses.

Her being a mother with two children came as a surprise but not a deterrent. Fact was, when she discussed her children, her face radiated with such affection that it only added fuel to the fire. "They're up at the cottage tormenting their grandparents for a week," she laughed.

She said she was dating some hotshot who owned a chain of carpet stores and drove a big Caddie, but I got the sense by the way she talked that their relationship wasn't serious. My instincts also told me she was very much attracted to me, and nothing was going to keep me from making her my lady.

I glanced at my watch: it was eight-fifteen. I had only a few minutes left, and I began to panic. "Well, Mrs. Cinderella," I said, "my time is running out. I guess, in a few minutes, I'll be spending the rest of the evening by myself." I tried to keep it light, but the thought of her leaving sent a dull ache through my body. I had to think fast. I had to find a way to woo her into staying. Then the words just came flowing out. "If you do me one huge favour, I promise I will love you for the rest of my life."

"What might that be?" she teased.

I pulled her gently to me and whispered, "I think we

belong together. This guy you're dating will never equal how special I can make you feel."

We nuzzled for a few seconds, and then she pulled away and stared into my eyes. "You're *really* smooth," she smiled and nodded that, yes, she would stay with me. We sat there for the next few moments in silence. Our hearts spoke sincerely to one another and made a covenant, and that night we became inseparable.

CHAPTER 25

Stand by Me

A year later Jackie and I had a no-frills wedding at City Hall. Did we live happily ever after? Much of the time yes, but there were periods when our relationship carried us deep into the eye of the storm, and fortunately a beautiful thing called love delivered us through. Adversity can either ruin a relationship or make it stronger. The fact that both of us had been through difficult times only served to make our marriage stronger. She'd been through a marriage with a husband who'd both physically and mentally abused her, and my life on the streets and in jail only made me appreciate Jackie and our marriage all the more.

Not everybody was happy with our marriage. One night, two weeks after our wedding, we met four friends for dinner, where we broke the news of our wedding. Two were shocked and suggested we should have just stayed living together, and another, who had been in an interracial marriage himself, contended that they seldom worked. I got a little uptight and reminded him that he loved Jack Daniels more than he did his wife and kids and that he had no right to compare our marriage to his. In the early 1970s, interracial marriages weren't nearly as common as they are today. But I also knew a lot of black and white same-race couples whose marriages had failed. Fortunately, neither Jackie nor I listened to their pearls of wisdom.

That's not to say we didn't experience racial bigotry along the way; we just refused to allow bigotry to manipulate us.

One night we decided to drop by a club where a couple of musician friends of mine had a gig. It was a bad move, and I knew it the second we entered the club and saw two burly bouncers at the front entrance. When they had guys that size working the door, it meant the place was crawling with rowdies.

As we entered, I cased the place and spotted half a dozen more bouncers roaming the floors. In the 1970s, there were many bars and clubs off the beaten track in Toronto where blacks dared not venture. Jackie, not having a racist bone in her body, was unaware of such dangers, but I should have followed my instincts and steered us back out. However, my macho pride wouldn't allow it.

The place was jammed, and people were standing five deep at the bar. We found an empty table near the back of the place, and then I headed to the bar to grab some drinks. It took about ten minutes to get served, and as I was shouldering my way back to the table I noticed this big guy leaning over Jackie. As I approached the table, he straightened up and looked me up and down. There was contempt written all over his face. I excused myself and brushed past, forcing him to take a few steps back. I set the drinks on the table without taking my eyes off him. He was tall, about six three, with broad shoulders, a thick neck, and a bit of a paunch. The stare-down lasted a few more seconds, and then he glanced at Jackie. "I'll give you a call sometime," he mumbled and gave me a sneer as he sauntered away, his shoulders rolling like he was the big dog in the house.

"What was that about?" I asked Jackie.

She squeezed my hand and leaned her head against my chest. "Can we go somewhere else?" she asked.

She was visibly upset, and it made me angry. It was obvious that he'd made some nasty comments to her. I didn't like where this thing was going. I began to mentally debate how to handle the situation. He was hanging with some guys near the bar.

"Did you have something going on with this guy at one time?" I asked her.

"No!" she snapped.

It was the first time in the six months we'd been dating that I'd seen her so upset.

"How come he's so uptight?" I asked.

She told me that he'd asked her out a few times, that she'd brushed him off, that his name was John.

I was getting an ugly message here. "What did he say to you?" I prodded.

She didn't want to answer.

I gently but firmly tilted her chin up and looked her in the eyes. "What did he say that got you so uptight?"

She returned my stare and paused for a few seconds. "He asked why I was dating a black guy when I wouldn't go out with him."

I knew there was more to it than that. "He called you a nigger lover! Didn't he?" I asked angrily.

She was trembling, and her eyes began to flood with tears. I picked up a napkin off the table and wiped them away.

"He called you a nigger lover, didn't he?" I repeated, this time more gently.

"Yes!" she blurted out, tears welling in her eyes.

I was in an instant rage, and I leapt out of my seat to confront him, but Jackie grabbed my arm and pleaded with me to forget it.

"Please, let's just go!"

But there was no way I was going to let this jerk slide. He was so stupid he didn't even know he'd violated a street code I was raised on by insulting my woman. I sat back down and pretended to be cool, but underneath I was steaming. "Forget this turkey," I said. "Let's just catch one set and go home. Okay?"

My comments relaxed her a bit. She had no idea that I'd already conceived an entirely different plan.

I noticed the guy was swilling back a lot of beer, which meant sooner or later he'd have to visit the washroom. It also meant his reflexes were deteriorating fast. Given a little more time, I knew I'd catch him alone, and then we'd see how courageous he was. I watched every move he made, how he shoved his way aggressively to the bar to order another beer, how he acted like he owned the place.

About half an hour later, I spotted him heading in our direction. He moved with the swagger and confidence guys his size often do. As he passed within a few feet of our table, he glanced over at us. I caught his eye and winked. He

slowed down, shot me a sneer, and then disappeared around
the corner. I couldn't wait to serve him up a plate of
vengeance, the main entree being a knuckle sandwich.

I reached into my jacket and pulled out the car keys, then
leaned over and whispered in Jackie's ear, "I don't feel too
cool in here anymore, sweetie, let's leave. I just have to hit
the john first. Can you bring the car to the side door?" I
asked and handed her the keys.

As I walked her to the side exit, she gave me a quizzical
look. She suspected something was up. "Honey, don't do
anything stupid," she pleaded.

"Don't worry, beautiful, I won't," I promised, then kissed
her on the cheek as I guided her to the door. I watched her
hurry toward the car, and then I turned and hustled down
the stairs.

I pushed the washroom door open and peeked inside,
and there was John, standing at the urinal, pulling his zipper
up. I quickly cased the surroundings; nobody else was
around. I crept up behind him and said, "Hey, big dog,
remember me?"

He was startled and wheeled around, his eyes glaring with
contempt. I appraised him quickly. He was at least two inches
taller and forty pounds heavier. Too big to get into a prolonged scuffle with. I knew I'd have to finish it fast. I feinted
as if I was turning to walk away and then pivoted back and
slammed a short left hook to his jaw. His head snapped back,
and his knees wobbled. I moved in quickly and tagged him
with a right, and he staggered back. I stepped in again and
threw a solid three-punch combination: a short right, a left
hook, and finally a right uppercut to the jaw. He was out cold
before his body sagged to the floor.

I grabbed him under the armpits, pulled him to the wall, and propped him up under one of the urinals. Then I calmly walked up the stairs, out the side door, and into the waiting car. I felt no guilt and no regret at the time. Any man who insults a woman in such a mean-spirited manner deserves to be brought down to size.

We went straight home and comforted one another. Long after Jackie had drifted off to sleep, I lay awake till the wee hours of the morning, partly lost in the serenity of the moment, during which I swore I'd protect her with my heart and soul, and partly reliving the events of the evening and admonishing myself for foolishly allowing some bigoted punk to take me to a place I no longer wanted to go.

I was angry with myself for violating the promise I'd made to myself about leaving the violent life behind. I also reminded myself that no matter where you lived there would always be bigots like him. They were like automated bowling pins: you knock one down, and a dozen others pop up. I had to develop more civilized ways of dealing with them. The thought of messing up my life, maybe ending up back behind bars and losing my home with Jackie over some loudmouthed, arrogant punk, frightened the hell out of me. I didn't want to spend a single night away from this woman, and I vowed never again to get suckered into a situation that could jeopardize what we had.

As far as the hassles of being in an interracial marriage go, some of our worst experiences have come from my own race, especially when we visited family in Detroit. One night we were at a house party in Detroit, and the music was cranked, and everybody was dancing and socializing and having a good time. I left Jackie on the sofa beside my sister Rose and headed to the kitchen to get some refreshments. My cousin Ronnie was there, and we got into a conversation.

A few minutes later, this very attractive sister strolled in and greeted Ronnie with a hug and a kiss on the cheek. "Who's your friend?" she asked, giving me the once-over, and, before he got the words out, she had squeezed in beside me, and her skirt slid up, exposing a pair of gorgeous ebony legs. "How come I haven't seen you around?" she asked. "I know most of Ronnie's people. I never saw you before."

"I live up in Toronto, so I don't get down here that much these days," I answered.

She shot me a flirtatious smile, checking me out. Suddenly, something prompted her to ask Ronnie, "Who's the paddy girl out in the living room?"

It was a spiteful remark, and I resented it. "Why? You got a problem with white folks?" I snapped.

She gave me a hostile look, as if I'd insulted her.

"That paddy girl happens to be my wife!" I informed her.

She glared at me in indignation. "How come all you brothers messing with white girls all the time?"

I told her I couldn't speak for the other brothers, but for me it wasn't about colour; to me, real love transcended race and culture.

But her venomous attitude didn't surprise me. Over the years, I've met many blacks who think that any brother who dates out of his race is a traitor. Perhaps it's true on many occasions, but I married my lady because I loved her. If she were black, Jewish, Latino, whatever, it wouldn't have made any difference to me. Anybody who dislikes my wife because of her race is missing out on a warm and loyal friend. We've survived more than twenty-five years of marriage through these troubled times, and that's cause for celebration.

One of the biggest obstacles in interracial marriages is family. Many parents don't approve of their sons or daughters marrying outside the race. One of the biggest concerns is having mixed grandchildren. Jackie and I were fortunate because both of our families accepted and supported us, although it wouldn't have mattered to either of us because we were both fiercely independent. My in-laws were a blessing, and we became very close. Unlike my family, which was large, they had only two children, both girls, and in time they viewed me as the son they never had. As for my family, every single one of them adores my wife.

I enjoyed being with Jackie and her children. It was the first time in many years that I felt a sense of belonging. Jimmy, the youngest, was three years old. He was sweet, fragile, and sensitive, and it took a little time for me to get close to him, but he's turned out to be a son and a man any father would be proud of. Shelly had a totally opposite personality. She was outgoing and took to me immediately and followed me around like a five o'clock shadow. We were also blessed with two beautiful children together, Clarence and Jennifer. They were all beautiful, friendly, and well-behaved children.

On the weekends, we'd go to places such as Wonderland, the zoo, the beach, and Ontario Place. We also enjoyed going on bike rides and to all-night drive-ins. Those early years, when the kids were young, were probably the happiest times of my life.

Being with Jackie often turned into an adventure. I never knew what to expect. Like one Friday evening. I came in from work, and she was sitting at the kitchen table with a newspaper and holding a yellow marker. I asked her what she was up to. She smiled and informed me that she'd entered me in a talent contest. You had to sing with a live band, and the winner would receive a dinner for two and a bottle of wine. That night I won performing Muhammad Ali's favourite tune, "Stand by Me," and after that Jackie was always entering me in one talent contest or another.

I also found that, through her love, the darkness of defeatism, anger, and depression that I'd been living under for so long was starting to lift, and old dreams were starting to stir again.

CHAPTER 26

Radio Dreams Reborn

One day the ownership of our company changed hands, and the new owner — a big, snarly, intimidating man named Bill Mack — dumped our general manager and assumed the position himself. Mack was a drunk, a tyrant, and unpredictable. Suddenly, I never knew from day to day what policies or rules would change. If we had a bad sales day, he'd freak out and call our sales staff — mostly kids in their late teens or early twenties — all kinds of derogatory names and force them to stay late to participate in sales meetings. Being the sales manager, I was supposed to conduct these stormy affairs, but his tantrums only served to heighten tensions and undermine my authority.

After the meetings, I sometimes had to go back to his suite at the Holiday Inn to supposedly discuss sales strategies. Usually, he'd get into a bottle of Crown Royal, and before long he'd be in a drunken stupor, slurring his words and telling me which frightened young kid I should blow out the door. On a couple of occasions, I came close to calling him out, but I played along because the money was good. When things got impossible, I'd remind myself of the good things in my life, that I'd be home shortly and cuddling with my wife on the sofa, that she'd ease the troubled waters of my emotions.

In spite of all the stress, the company was actually flourishing. It opened a new division, which canvassed industrial areas of major cities around southern Ontario with kitchenwares, ladies' nylons, cheap jewellery, cookbooks, and dictionaries. But with rapid expansion came longer hours and ever more pressure to produce. Many times I didn't get out of the office until after eight o'clock. Then Bill began demanding that I work weekends training part-timers and checking inventory. Soon the bad days began to outnumber the good ones.

The frustrations of my job began to spill over into my personal life. I'd drag myself home each night tired to the bone and too stressed out to enjoy Jackie and the kids. I was moody and uptight for allowing this tyrant to treat my staff as if they were dirt. In the mornings, it became a chore to drag myself to the office to face another day with him.

One afternoon it really hit the fan when Bill forced me to pink-slip six sales people, one of whom was a kid named Rob, whom I'd promoted to assistant sales manager. The poor kid thought he'd finally got his life on track, and he was away on his honeymoon and didn't have a clue he'd have no job when he got back. Two other salespeople had supposedly violated a new company policy: no fraternizing on the job. They were twenty-year-old kids on the same crew and had dated and fallen in love. I pleaded their case with Bill, but nothing could change his mind. When I broke the news to them, they wept like babies. It took every ounce of my strength to contain my own tears. I deeply cared for these kids, and they'd looked up to me as both mentor and friend. It was at that moment I decided I could no longer work for someone like that.

My wife is a very perceptive person, and when I walked through the door that evening she picked up on my emotional state. I cried on her shoulder about how miserable my job had become. I said that I felt like a traitor for sacrificing my values just to keep a damn job. After I settled down, she suggested I look for another job. "Doing what?" I thought to myself. With my criminal record, most firms wouldn't have taken a gamble on me. The thought of leaving my job filled me with desperation. "Where will I go from here?"

That evening Jackie began hinting about me going back to school. "No way! That's never going to happen," I thought, and I brushed the idea away. But I underestimated her resolve. When her mind's made up, she never lets go.

A few nights later, we were watching TV, and out of the blue she asked me, if I could have the choice of doing any type of job, what it would be. It was a good question. It made me think. "A radio announcer," I finally said. Then I shared with her the story about the time when I was twelve and saw Alan Freed at the Windsor Arena introducing all those great acts. I told her how I'd met Buddy Holly, Chuck Berry, and even Freed himself briefly, how I'd begun to dream one night about becoming a radio personality like Alan, and how my friends had laughed when I told them about it.

"Honey," Jackie said, placing her arms around me and

gently stroking the back of my neck. "You know so much about music and sports, and you've got tons of charisma and a gift of gab that won't quit. You'd be great in radio."

She believed in me so much, and it lifted my spirits. For the first time in years, I began to entertain those old thoughts of getting into radio. The trouble was I didn't have a clue how to pursue my dream.

But Jackie did.

One night I came home, and she was at the living room table studying a pile of brochures and pamphlets from various colleges around the city; she'd spent the day scouting these places. She was starting to plant ideas . . . slowly.

A few weeks later, I came home to another surprise. "Hi, honey," she smiled and kissed me. She had this happy glow on, so I knew something was up. "I made you an appointment with a guidance counsellor at Seneca College." I didn't have the heart to say no, so I faked an appreciative smile and hugged her, but inside I cringed. I knew in my heart that going back to school at my age and with my background was out of the question.

Then things finally blew up with Bill. A kid had not made his daily sales quota, and Bill had been drinking, and he threatened to take the kid out back and thrash him. The poor kid was so scared that he raced out of the boardroom.

That did it! The pent-up anger and frustration in me exploded. I smashed my fist on the table and yelled, "Damn you, Bill, if you're looking to pound on somebody, why don't you try me?"

His face went white with shock; then, after a few seconds, he began to move toward me, his eyes squinting as if he was crazed.

"You come one step closer," I warned, "and we're going to get it on!"

He stopped and glared at me, and the room went deathly silent. Then he spun around and stormed out, slamming the door so hard that a painting fell off the wall. After he left, I went and dismissed *all* the salespeople; then I walked past his office, tossed my office keys on his desk, and quit for good!

The next few weeks were very difficult. It was the first time in almost four years I was out of legitimate work. Jackie helped me put a résumé together, and I made a ton of copies and distributed and mailed them to sales companies across southern Ontario. Being a solid sales person and a three-time Golden Gloves champion, I figured my credentials might open a few doors. I figured wrongly!

After a dozen interviews, I began to get the picture: most prime sales positions went to white people with university degrees. I might have been a heavyweight on the streets and in the ring, but in the corporate world my grade four education made me a ninety-pound weakling.

Unemployment left me restless, and with time on my hands I started hanging again with some old contacts. Word got around that I was in the market for a payday, and offers started floating my way: a bookie I knew offered me a spot with him chasing down bets; a guy who owned pinball and slot machines wanted me to strong-arm small businesses into taking his machines; an old loan shark friend asked me to collect delinquent accounts for him. One of my old boxing associates even offered me a gig in his male escort service. The money was good — the only thing was that, at the end of the night, I was expected to do the dirty deed, which violated my newfound principles and meant cheating on my wife. I wouldn't have messed up my marriage for all the money in the world.

Then, about two months into my unemployment, I bumped into an old friend, who told me that the Drake Hotel was looking for a DJ in the lounge. The Drake was one of the city's seediest dumps and a known drug den. It was a dark and gloomy place and a social club for pimps, prostitutes, drug dealers, crack heads, and various other flotsam of the underworld. The second I entered the joint my instincts warned me of trouble, but when the money is funny sometimes any job will have to do.

I took the gig, but right away I knew I was going to have trouble because, for a place that catered to such a tough crowd, there was only one bouncer, if you could have called him that. Whenever trouble broke out, he vanished. And you could always count on a crap game going on in the washroom. In fact, there were probably more crap games going on in there than there was actual crapping. I watched an endless stream of shady deals going down in the shadows of that place, but my gig was to spin the sounds, not to get into the private affairs of the hustlers.

On my first night on the job, two guys got into a vicious brawl in the middle of the dance floor. I was minding my own business behind the bar spinning the jams when the owner, Gino, came rushing over and pleaded with me to break it up. I asked him where the hell the bouncer was, and he threw his arms up in frustration; he didn't know. Like a damned fool, I hopped over the bar and pulled the combatants apart.

One of them took exception and swung at me. I side-stepped the punch and administered a choke hold, using just enough pressure to subdue him. A bouncer worth his salt will try to defuse a situation by talking guys down rather than punching them out. Violence only serves to challenge their manhood, and there's a good chance they'll be looking for some payback.

A few nights later, another fight broke out, and again Gino came begging me to break it up. I asked him how much he was paying this so-called bouncer for a night's work.

Gino said, "Seventy-five dollars a night."

Here he was paying this dude good coin, and *I was doing his job.* "Fire him!" I said, and that night the title of bouncer was added to my portfolio. After that, it got so bad that some nights I'd spend more time breaking up fights than spinning music.

One night I came home with my face covered in cuts and bruises and my shirt ripped and stained with blood, and, at the sight of me, Jackie burst into tears. It broke my heart to see her so upset. She pleaded with me to quit before something serious happened, so, to appease her, I promised to look for another gig, but the truth was I was making $450 a week, and there was no place else I could pull in that kind of dough.

I never discussed the dangers of the job with her, how it was becoming more threatening each night, because I knew doing so would just upset her even more. When you break up fights and ban violent people, you tend to make enemies. She didn't know that some junked-up dope dealer had pulled a blade on me one night and threatened to cut me. I never told her how my life had been threatened on other occasions.

One night I was breaking up a fight on the dance floor when a small-time chump named Santo crept up behind me and blind-sided me with a couple of punches to the face. He was just a punk kid whom I could have licked in my sleep, and he didn't do any damage, but I'd made another enemy. A few nights later, I had to bar him, and he freaked on me and began making threats, said we'd settle it after closing. When I left, he was nowhere to be seen, but I knew he was now just another crazy carrying a grudge against me.

A few days later, I went to work to find Gino sitting at the bar sucking up to Santo. Gino waved me over and informed me that Santo had apologized for his past behaviour, so Gino had lifted his ban. I kept my cool, but inside I was doing a slow burn. To allow Santo back on the premises only served to make my job even more dangerous. I didn't have to wait long for that prophecy to be fulfilled.

A few weeks later, yet another fight broke out, and as I was breaking it up somebody sucker-punched me once again in the face: Santo! This time I snatched him by the lapels of his leather jacket and brought my forehead down and head-butted him hard, squarely on the nose, and blood began gushing from it like a geyser. Then I jerked him up and slammed him hard against the wall, and I dragged him to the front door with his heels sliding along the floor, and I tossed him onto the sidewalk, like you see in old western movies. As I turned back inside the lounge, I had to walk through the crowd of bystanders that had gathered in the front lobby, and I heard a couple of threats growled in my direction.

I knew that my luck wouldn't hold out forever if I continued this crazy gig, that eventually some demented dude would stab or shoot me. Some gutless punk like Santo. On the drive home that night, a sense of foreboding came over me as I thought about my encounter with Santo. He'd gotten what he deserved, but I drew no satisfaction from what I'd done. I'd broken the promise I'd made to myself that the violent chapter of my life was closed forever. My sense of unease grew, and it occurred to me that maybe fate had other plans for me, that my life was destined to end as tragically as those of my cousins Sonny and Leroy had.

I couldn't shake the feeling . . . but I needed the money.

CHAPTER 27

The Spider's Web

One night everything came to a head at the Drake Hotel with a dangerous pimp named Cool Breeze. He wasn't in Santo's Mickey Mouse league: Cool Breeze was pure thug, and he had all the other pimps and hustlers well intimidated. He was also known to brutally shake down the hookers for their cash.

I was behind the bar selecting some tunes one night when I heard screams coming from the ladies' washroom, just around the corner from my booth. I hopped the bar and rushed into the washroom to find Cool Breeze with a tiny white girl backed up against the wall. He was slapping her hard across the face. She couldn't have been more than seventeen, and I wondered how she'd even got past the front door. Her nose was bleeding, and the look of terror in her eyes made my blood boil.

I grabbed Cool Breeze by the shoulder and spun him around hard against the door. Only a naïve fool would have taken his eyes off somebody as treacherous as Cool Breeze, even for a split second, but that's exactly what I did. The girl was sobbing and shaking, so I held the door open for her to leave, and, as she rushed by me, Cool Breeze brought a blade flashing out of his pants pocket.

He began waving the knife at me, taunting me. "I'm going to cut your black ass up real good nigger," he said, and he had a reputation for doing exactly that. The deranged glint in his eye that told me he was for real.

I had to act quickly. I tried to talk him down while, at the same time, edging toward the door, but he read my mind and moved to block my escape. The only other way out was through a window, which meant turning my back. That would have been suicide.

He lunged wildly at me, and I jumped back, the blade missing my chest by only inches. He let out a burst of insane laughter and then lunged at me again. I retreated as far back as possible until I bumped into the sink. He had me cornered! He growled, "I told you not to be messing in my business, nigger! Now you got to pay!"

As he moved forward again, my right foot bumped into something. I glanced down and saw that it was a sturdy metal trash can. In one quick motion, I jerked it up and hurled it full force at his forehead. The blow made a solid clang, and it sent him flying backward. He went flat on his back and lay there motionless. All kinds of thoughts began racing through my mind. First relief, then fear. Had I killed him?

Then the washroom door flew open, and Gino and two uniformed cops came rushing in. Before I could say anything, they ordered me against the wall. One of them bent over to examine Cool Breeze. At least he was alive. They called an ambulance to cart him to the hospital, and they took me to the police station, where they held me for questioning for a couple of hours and then let me go. Cool Breeze ended up with a concussion and ligament damage to his neck, which at least meant that he'd be slowed up some in the future.

On the drive home that night, I came to the full realization that Cool Breeze had actually intended to kill me, especially after the cops told me that his rap sheet included doing time for a previous conviction of attempted murder. I was tired of living in fear. Jackie's suggestion about going back to school began to sound like heaven compared to this hell.

It seemed like the only way out of this sad state of affairs. So it was good-bye Drake Lounge and hello school.

To be accepted into the broadcast journalism course at Seneca College, I first had to take a battery of tests. The results were less than flattering, and it was decided that I required two semesters of college prep first. It may sound weird that someone would be more terrified going back to the classroom than he'd been during street fights, gang wars, and jail, but that's how it was for me. For me, the classroom had become a symbol of failure. The very thought of returning brought old memories of rejection and ineptness flooding back. Memories of all the taunts and put-downs that had been buried deep in my past. All those built-up fears scared the hell out of me!

Except for a twist of fate, I would have quit school before I'd even started again.

It was 1979, I was thirty years old, and I'd been out of

school for fifteen years. Most of my new classmates were in their late teens and early twenties and seemed to be full of excitement and energy. I felt out of place in their world, and, although I tried to will myself to relax, it wasn't working. I was stressed and in a constant cold sweat. And those two old predators were back — self-doubt and lack of self-esteem. I could hear negative voices whispering in my mind: *"You've got to get the hell out of this place! It's not for you!"*

On my very first day in class, I gave up. I rose from my seat and eased my way to the door as inconspicuously as possible. I was about to bolt down the hallway when I felt a hand on my shoulder.

"Where you going?"

I wheeled around to face the voice, and I looked into a pair of penetrating blue eyes.

"Hi, Spider! I'm Doug Harris, the English teacher."

I had no idea how he knew who I was or why he'd stopped me. Now I tend to think of it as a blessing. If he hadn't intervened in my life, I would never have stayed in school.

"Where are you off to?" he asked.

I wasn't in the mood for sermons. "Another one of these do-good saints," I thought. But there was something sincere about him that caught me off guard. He folded his arms across his chest, his eyes never wavering from mine. We stood in awkward silence for a few tense seconds. All kinds of thoughts were racing through my mind. "What's this dude's story?" I wondered.

"Are you giving up so soon?" he asked, his eyes fixed on mine.

"This isn't for me!" I shot back defiantly.

"How do you know? You haven't tried it yet," he said calmly. Before I could respond, he continued. "It appears to me as though you're quitting."

What he said was the brutal truth, and it stung like a slap in the face. I thought about my wife and how she'd held my hand so tightly as we'd walked to my car that morning. Of how she'd waved with excitement as I'd driven off. If I quit now I'll probably have spent the rest of my life wondering if I could ever have made it in the radio business.

"Spider," he said, placing his hand on my shoulder. "I saw you fight at Maple Leaf Gardens a few years back, and I know it takes a tremendous amount of courage and determination to climb into the ring. Why not devote some of that same determination to this project? I've got a feeling you'll do okay."

His words made me think hard. Here was this stranger reaching out to me. He had a lot more confidence in me than I did. Nothing else was said. We simply turned around and went back into the classroom, and I thought, "This man might have just saved my life."

During those first weeks, I continued to get overwhelming urges to bail out, but thanks to the support of Doug Harris I gradually grew to feel at ease, and things began to happen. Slowly, I buried my past, and a new future began to emerge and with it a real desire to gain knowledge.

It was during this period that I began to look squarely at my inner feelings, which in turn brought me to a clearer understanding of how my low self-esteem had undermined me. I began to understand that my negative feelings were an illusion, a state of mind. I'd been labelled early as a slow learner, and I'd been programmed to think I was stupid and therefore didn't deserve to dream big. It took time, determination, and thought, but with the support of others I was able to win my battle against my own lack of confidence.

One of the areas in which I began to excel was writing. For that, much of the credit goes to an extraordinary writing teacher named Mrs. Margaret Hauser. She passed away a few years after I graduated — but not before planting the seeds of hope deep within me. With the exception of my wife, this sweet elderly lady inspired and challenged me more than any person I've ever known. I had rarely discussed my past with anyone except Jackie, but over time, after I got to know and respect Mrs. Hauser, I opened up and shared my life with her. She was genuinely fascinated by it. We engaged in many stimulating conversations and often got into debates.

As my confidence grew, I began to share my personal dream of becoming a radio personality with her. She strongly encouraged me but also implored me never to change my style. It was through her countless hours of mentoring that my mind gradually changed, and I began to believe that my dream was possible. Because of this saintly woman, the spirit of mentoring dwells in my soul today. It is because of her that I try to give back to society. Without her guidance, and the love and support of my beautiful wife, I would not have finished school and would not have lived my dream.

One time I wrote a book report on the Tennessee Williams play *A Streetcar Named Desire*, and Mrs. Hauser gave me an A+. She told the class that it was the first time she'd ever given any student such a high grade. For the record, grading only goes as high as A in college. Even while handing it to me, she assured me that my chances of getting another A+ were remote.

I took it as a challenge and responded by writing my final essay on "The History of Cover Version Music" because of my passion for R&B music. I spent countless hours in the library researching the true history of pop music, and I wrote about the long list of black entertainers whose music had been ripped off by greedy record producers — black and white. My efforts paid off: I got another A+!

But not everybody was in my corner on my return to school. One night, halfway through my first semester, Top Cat and a couple of old gang members breezed into town from Detroit on "business," and they wanted to get together. I had an important school assignment due the next morning, which included an interview I'd just done with Rick Vaive, the captain of the Toronto Maple Leafs at the time, so I was reluctant. But Top Cat could be pretty persuasive, and I relented.

We met at a restaurant in Chinatown and shared some laughs, had a few drinks, and reminisced about the good old days. But the funny thing was, looking back then, I wondered what had been so good about them. At about eleven-thirty, Top Cat suggested we hit a few of the downtown clubs. I told him I'd have to take a pass, that I had to get back to the crib to finish some homework.

He immediately began to badger me. "Brother!" he said, his face breaking into a sneer of scorn. "Forget that dumb-assed school shit! You too old to be thinking about that shit!" Then he reached into his pocket, pulled out a hefty roll of bills, and said, "This is what it's about — *money!*"

Top Cat was a prime example of most of the guys who'd

grown up on my turf who were being held hostage by the limitations of their minds. Debating him would have been pointless. He'd been programmed to believe manhood comes from fancy clothes, jewellery, expensive automobiles, busting heads, and making babies. He lacked the vision to understand how important education was in my scheme of things. He didn't get it! He didn't know I'd found a new guiding principle: *it's not where you've come from in life but where you're going that counts!*

Top Cat's negative comments only served to strengthen my resolve. Nothing outside of an act of God could have deterred me from completing college and pursuing my dream and turning it into reality.

That was the last time I'd see Top Cat for close to fifteen years. Three months later, he was sentenced to ten years in the Jackson, Michigan state pen for assault. The last I heard of him he was out in L.A. and was heavy into drugs.

For three long years, I worked at various night jobs — mostly taking janitorial work — and kept at my studies during the day, but when I finally graduated in 1981 it was with honours. I made the Dean's List and won the Board of Governors Award as well as landed a couple of literary scholarships.

Graduation night was among the proudest moments of my life. I became the first person in my family to graduate from college. Later that night, Jackie asked me what had been going through my mind as I'd accepted my diploma. The answer to her question was many thoughts, the most prominent being that I'd beaten the odds and silenced the critics who'd written me off. "Not bad," I thought, "for

someone who had been diagnosed early with a learning disability and a behavioural problem."

But my battle wasn't over. In some ways, it had only begun: now I had to land a job. In spite of my high grades, my academic accomplishments, the awards I had won, and the time I had spent apprenticing with cable TV stations and newspapers, getting a gig in the radio field was proving difficult. In the first few weeks after graduation, I sent out close to a hundred résumés and demo tapes to radio stations across Canada. The results were depressing. If I got responses at all, they were usually form letters: *Thank you for your interest in our organization; however, at this time there is nothing available in your particular area. Good luck.*

On the few occasions I managed to get interviews, nothing came of them. After almost a year with no radio job on the radar, I began to have second thoughts about my choice of career. The ominous words uttered by my friends so many years before started to ring prophetically true once again: "Nigger, you talkin' like a damn fool. Can't nobody black be no DJ on the ray-dyo." The truth was, when it came to Canada, they were pretty much right! Even by the '80s few men of colour got anywhere in Canada's media monopolies.

Either I had to be ready for the fight of my life to make my dream happen, or I'd have to bail on myself.

Because of the lack of people of colour in the media, I knew I'd have to be subtle in my approach, careful not to offend anybody, a tough task when you're dealing with thin-skinned, hypocritical, and pompous so-called pillars of the business community. Often, when a black man comes right out and makes these types of comments, he is accused of that same old tired shtick about playing the race card, but so many of the media in Canada in the 1980s lived in denial. Racism? In the United States, yes, of course, but here in Canada? No way! That was the prevailing attitude.

I fought hard to keep a positive spin on things. Whether I was dealing with closed minds or not, I'd come too far to allow anyone to get me off my game plan.

Over the next few years, I learned a lot about how the media work. It's not always the most talented and creative people who land the prime gigs but often those with contacts. Fortunately, from my sales background, I knew that rejection just goes with the territory, and after a while I became impervious to it. Still, I knew that I required one more very significant element in my corner: Lady Luck! I desperately needed to feel her embrace . . . and soon!

What I got instead wasn't Lady Luck but George Chuvalo, who wasn't nearly as good looking but who turned out to be a far more loyal and valuable ally.

One afternoon during the late summer of 1983, I was having lunch with George and griping about my difficulties trying to get my foot in the media door. He told me that he'd been approached to host a syndicated boxing series on TV called *Famous Knockouts* and that the producer was searching for another person to cohost with him. He promised to recommend me.

True to his word, big George called me the next day; he had set up an appointment for me with the producer. The thought of cohosting a boxing show sent my heart soaring. Wow! I'd get a gig on TV with one of my best friends and in my own field! What a start! It couldn't get much better!

But it took me only a few moments after arriving at the studio to scope the picture: the producer had only agreed to meet with me to pacify George. He said he was looking for someone with broadcasting experience and a high profile. I was never under consideration. Not even an audition!

That evening I called Chuvalo and had to give him the news about how badly it had gone down. Big George was upset and assured me that he'd get on it. Bright and early the next morning, the producer of the show called and said he wanted to meet with me again — urgently. Two weeks later, I was cohosting *Famous Knockouts* syndicated nationwide with Chuvalo.

George never mentioned a word about how he'd gone to bat for me, but I got the whole story during a wrap party months later that he'd threatened to walk if I didn't get the job. I will always be indebted to George for his friendship and confidence. He came through for me big-time. That television show with him was what finally opened the doors to the media for me.

A few weeks after the show was aired, I landed a gig as a sports and entertainment writer for a small publication. Then, in 1987, I started a late-night dedication call-in show on CHWO radio in Oakville, just west of Toronto. It was the first time *The Spider's Web* went on air. Listeners called me to request particular songs, just as I'd listened to callers request songs from Alan Freed way back in the 1950s.

I even developed a prerecorded intro to my show. It's a funky little audio pastiche that I put together myself and that always gives me an inward little smile of satisfaction when it comes on. It begins with a trumpet fanfare and a drum roll, followed by the Coasters version of "And Along Came Jones," then me saying "It's good to be me" with a little giggle and then — quoting an old expression from the streets of Detroit — "Hey, baby, ain't nuthin' shakin' but the bacon." Finally, the soulful thump-budda-thump beat of James Brown's theme song, "Night Train," breaks in along with the sound of a trolley bell ding-dinging.

The dream that I'd first dreamt as a skinny twelve-year-old kid back in 1959 — and that I'd buried for almost thirty years — had finally come true. I had beaten those two predators — lack of confidence and lack of self-esteem — and, for the first time in my life, felt as though I was stepping out of the darkness and into the sunlight. Finally, my future looked bright.

I had done it!

Epilogue

These days I'm hosting *The Spider's Web* on Canada's largest AM station, CFRB 1010 in Toronto. I'm also hosting another syndicated TV boxing show with George Chuvalo called *Famous Fights*, which has been getting a lot of airplay.

My radio career has brought me many rewards and has allowed me to cross paths with many fascinating people. Here are just a few:

In 1988, I heard that Chubby Checker was coming to town. Checker was called the Twist King, and "The Twist" was the only tune to go to number one twice on the Billboard charts by the same artist: first in September of 1960, then again in January of 1962. Checker was going to be doing his thing at the Royal York Hotel, and Gino Empry, who booked talent at the Imperial Room there, set up the interview for me. I almost blew everything in the first few seconds when I asked Chubby if there was any truth to the allegations that he'd stolen "The Twist" from Detroit singer Hank Ballard, who'd written and recorded it first. He got so upset I thought he was going to jump up and throw down on me. "Man, why do people keep bringing up this old crap?" I managed to settle him down, and we had a good interview, but it showed me just how careful I had to be around big-name personalities.

I also did personal interviews that year with Martha Reeves, Brenda Lee, Wilson Pickett, Roy Orbison, Bo Diddley, Ben E. King, Smokey Robinson, The Temptations, and many more. I also emceed the Freedom Festival, a major

Windsor–Detroit-area event in which I was guest of honour in the parade opening the festival.

That year I hosted the Toronto Sports Dinner of the Year at the Royal York Hotel. Special guests included Muhammad Ali and Lennox Lewis, who had just won the Olympic gold medal for Canada in Korea. I had the good fortune to become friends with Lennox many years before he became heavyweight champion of the world.

One of my most memorable times dealing with show-biz people was in 1991 when I toured with Charlie Hodge, one of Elvis Presley's best friends. Charlie was the guy who'd handed Elvis his scarves and water on stage during the televised 1968 comeback special. He'd also lived with the Presleys at Graceland for seventeen years, and, because he was an accomplished musician, he'd played sheet music onto tapes so that Elvis could learn the tunes.

That summer I travelled throughout Ontario, Michigan, and western New York opening for Charlie and his twelve-piece Elvis tribute band. My job as emcee was to warm up the audience with some '50s and '60s tunes and jokes and then introduce Charlie. After most shows, we'd sit around and jam, and Charlie would share memories of his years with Elvis.

One night Charlie suddenly disappeared and returned five minutes later with his arms loaded with videos. Over the next few hours, we sat around watching the private, behind-the-scenes antics of Elvis and the Memphis Mafia. The one scene that will always stand out in my mind is of the guys having a quiet party in the recreation room at Graceland. With them, of course, is a bevy of beautiful ladies. Charlie is sitting with this one lady, and she keeps asking where Elvis

is. Charlie keeps telling her not to worry, that Elvis will be
there soon. Suddenly, Elvis appears in the door, and the
camera follows him as he nonchalantly strolls over and
parks himself next to Hodge and the lady. At first, the
woman isn't aware that Elvis has entered or that he's just sat
down beside her, but when she turns and comes face to face
with Elvis he flashes his pearly whites and says, "Hi, I'm
Elvis," and the lady actually faints and keels right over! Man!
Who else had *that* kind of effect on people?

I felt privileged to be viewing Charlie's private collection
of videos of this larger-than-life figure called Elvis. While we
watched, Charlie never uttered a word. He just sat quietly
sipping his Jack Daniels and staring into the screen. I suppose he was reliving those days. On a couple of occasions,
tears rolled down his cheeks. It was obvious the man had
loved Elvis very much.

Since I was a huge Elvis fan, hanging with Charlie Hodge
was the ultimate journey in nostalgia for me. They were
some great times.

In 1992, I was the keynote speaker at the International
Boxing Hall of Fame Awards in New York. At the head table
was Muhammad again, plus Archie Moore, Jake Lamotta,
Jersey Joe Walcott, Kid Gavilan, and Billy Conn, all great
champions. It was a humbling experience to be at the head
of such a table of champions.

In 1994, I was presented with the Easter Seals Award for
my charitable work. I also began receiving many invitations
to appear as a motivational speaker. These days I speak on
self-esteem all over North America. I love sharing my stories
and experiences with young people.

In 1996, I was inducted into the Canadian Boxing Hall of

Fame as a journalist and commentator. It was a huge thrill and honour, one I wish my father could have seen. I thought of him a lot that night. That year also brought another unexpected award: Don King Productions surprised me with the 1996 Canadian Boxing Commentator of the Year Award.

About that time, I also got to know Rubin "Hurricane" Carter. Intense would be an understatement in describing Rubin. He is one of the most enigmatic people I've ever met. One day he'd be full of laughter, and the next day he'd be silent and serious. It was as though he had many burdens on his mind, which I guess he did considering that he'd spent so many years in prison for a crime he claimed he never committed. One day he looked so distant that I felt compelled to ask what was troubling him. "I miss the blackness of New Jersey," he said. He was living in Canada then, and I understood exactly where he was coming from. We often discussed issues that blacks face. The only thing that bothers me is that after his book and much-acclaimed movie came out — *The Hurricane* — he stopped returning my calls. Where are you, Hurricane? You're still my man.

My music career also took off. I began opening for some big nostalgia acts: Gerry and the Pacemakers, Peter Noone of Herman's Hermits, Billy J. Kramer, and the Hollies, among many others. Those were big thrills!

Also, in 1997, I began a tradition each April of hosting the Shaw Festival Night of Boxing at Toronto's Royal York Hotel. It became an annual evening of professional boxing to raise funds for the festival. At a thousand dollars a seat, this prestigious event is attended each spring by a well-heeled corporate clientele, and it has raised almost two million dollars.

I was also fortunate to get to know Cito Gaston back in the mid-'90s when he was managing the Toronto Blue Jays those years they were winning the pennants. Cito was the first black manager in major-league history to win a World Series. You'd think that with all his accomplishments he'd have been selected, at least once, as manager of the year. I believe that many of the members of the Baseball Writers Association and its old boys' network had their noses stuck so far up the butts of Sparky Anderson, Tommy Lasorda, and Tony La Russa that they could never be objective when it came to Cito's accomplishments.

Just after I became friends with Cito, things heated up between him and the Toronto media over his suggestions that certain Toronto media members were racist. I guess months of hearing the same tired old wisecracks got to him, and he reacted. Like him, I believed that much of the criticism was mean spirited and even cowardly, but racially motivated? I wasn't so sure. Nevertheless, I defended Cito many times on my radio show, and he appreciated the support.

Another courageous athlete I met about that time and became friends with was Tie Domi, the one-of-a-kind enforcer for the Toronto Maple Leafs. I met Tie in 1996 when I was ring announcer at a Billy "The Kid" Irwin fight. Domi was with Doug Gilmour — another of my favourite athletes — and they invited me to join them afterward. Being a huge hockey fan, I quickly accepted their invitation. I respect hockey players; many, like Tie, are warriors to the bone, and I have a deep respect for fighters. I was surprised to find that Tie dislikes discussing his rink pugilistic exploits and would rather talk boxing. Over the past few years, I've had the pleasure of working with him on some health club and sports bar grand openings. He's an inspiring guy. He was a kid who dreamed of making it to the NHL, but people just patted him on the shoulder and said, "Yeah, good luck," because most thought he was too small. However, through sheer determination and the will to win, he made his dream a reality. I admire Tie for many reasons, but the most compelling is his huge heart and commitment to always be the best he can be.

One of my proudest achievements came in 2002 when I was the recipient of the Premier of Ontario's Award for my work in the field of arts and entertainment. Not long after that, in 2003, I received an Ontario government appointment as travelling ambassador for the province's Youth Apprenticeship Skilled Labour Program.

But my most gratifying experiences now happen during my motivational speaking engagements. There is nothing more fulfilling than planting the seeds of hope in the hearts of youth and watching those seeds begin to blossom. My mission in life now is to inspire others to pursue their dreams until they become reality.

As long as I draw breath, I will battle lack of self-esteem — and drive it out of the minds of our youth. I tell kids: *Fate is what life gives you. Destiny is what you do with it.*

I survived the streets by being ruthless and violent, but I overcame them through love, compassion, and education.

Acknowledgements

Out of the Darkness is dedicated to all those wonderful people who believed in me.

Let me begin with the most special of all, my wife, Jackie Robinson Jones. She is the one person in my lifetime who has managed to ease the troubled waters of my emotions. She is my dearest friend and the most cherished gift God has bestowed on me. It was through her love and inspiration that I eventually chased my dream of becoming a radio personality into reality. Without her, there would be no happy ending to this story.

I would also like to dedicate *Out of the Darkness* to my four awesome children: Shelly, Jennifer, Jimmy, and Clarence, who were forced to live with me through some hard times. Yet it was through their precious lives that I somehow managed to move out of the darkness and into the light.

I am also profoundly grateful to my friend Michael Hughes for the hours he devoted to helping me to organize my life story and get it down on paper. Without his dedication, encouragement, and writing skills, this book would never have been written.

Much of my success also has to do with loyalty and friendships. No one has given more in this department than my main man, George Chuvalo. Thanks for opening the doors of opportunity for me, Champ. You showed deep faith in my ability when others didn't have a clue what the Spider was all about. It was through your painful experiences, the loss of so many loved ones, that I learned the meaning of true courage. We've had some great times during the production of our two TV series — *Famous Knockouts* and *Famous Fights*. At times, we laughed so hard the crew thought we'd gone insane. With God's grace, there'll be more of the same laughter.

Out of the Darkness is also dedicated to all those who have dreams. To them, I say seek out the encouragement and confidence it takes to bring them into reality. Remember, *"It's not where you've come from but where you're going that counts."*

Working in the media has been an exciting and rewarding experience, and over the years it has afforded me glorious opportunities to meet some nice people in the industry. It's because of their support that I hung in through some stormy weather.

Michael Landsberg, the eloquent and often provocative host of TSN's hit talk show *Off the Record*, comes to mind. We've been in some fiery debates over the years. Maybe that's the reason I keep getting invited back so often. The show has given me tremendous exposure. Thanks, Mike.

I also owe many thanks to other industry people: Pat Marsden, John Derringer, Mike Hogan, Joe Tilley, John Oakley, Ian Grant, Todd Hayes, Bob Mackowycz Jr., John Gallagher, Greg Sansone, my protégé George Stromboulopoulos, and of course the "Rain Man" Mike Damergis, who hooked me up with the Fox Radio Network. And I cannot forget my dear friends Liam Maguire and Dave Johnson. Each of these talented individuals has helped my career to take flight. It has been a privilege to work with each one of them.

I also owe a tremendous amount of gratitude to Gary

Slaight, president of Standard Broadcasting. He is truly a man of vision. When I first arrived at CFRB a few years back, the audience was predominantly white. Yet he had the courage and foresight to open the door and invite an outspoken brother into the fold. Also thanks to Program Manager Steve Kowch for his support and confidence in giving me a dynamite time slot.

I will remain eternally grateful to Mr. Bob Mackowycz Sr. To me, you are as special as it gets, and I will always hold you in the highest esteem. Thank you for opening the door at FAN 590. Your confidence in me was unrelenting. When others made promises they had no intention of keeping, your word was enough to seal the deal.

One other person whose courage has had a tremendous impact on me is a guy named Joseph Pampena. Better known as J.P., he lost his sight at age 25 after a negative reaction to penicillin. This tragic event did not prevent him from becoming one of the finest publicists I've had the honor of working with. Thanks, J.P., for all your confidence and friendship.

Finally, I would like to give props to all the producers and engineers who have worked diligently with me behind the scenes. You are unsung and underpaid for your efforts.